COOKING WITH A PASSION FOR PORK

pig

DUNCAN BAIRD PUBLISHERS

LONDON

COOKING WITH A PASSION FOR PORK

pig

Johnnie Mountain

Pig
Johnnie Mountain

First published in the United Kingdom and Ireland in
2012 by Duncan Baird Publishers Ltd
Sixth Floor, Castle House, 75–76 Wells Street
London W1T 3QH

Conceived, created and designed by Duncan Baird
Publishers

Managing Editor: Grace Cheetham
Editor: Nicola Graimes
Recipe Tester: Caroline Brewester
Art Direction and Designer: Manisha Patel
Production: Uzma Taj
Commissioned Photography: Yuki Sugiura
Food Stylist: Johnnie Mountain with Aya Nishimura
Prop Stylist: Cynthia Inions
Videography: Yuki Sugiura and Film Infinity

British Library Cataloguing-in-Publication Data:
A CIP record for this book is available from the
British Library

ISBN: 978-1-84899-036-4

10 9 8 7 6 5 4 3 2 1

Typeset in Nexus Mix
Colour reproduction by XY Digital
Printed in China by Imago

NOTES ON THE RECIPES
Unless otherwise stated:
• All recipes serve 4
• Use medium eggs, fruit and vegetables
• Use fresh ingredients, including herbs and chillies
• Do not mix metric and imperial measurements
• 1 tsp = 5ml   1 tbsp = 15ml   1 cup = 250 ml

CONTENTS

INTRODUCTION

My greatest childhood memory is definitely my Nana Olga's bacon butty; running to her house after school, mouth watering in anticipation of the hand-cut, smoky, crisp bacon sandwiched between two slices of soft brown, doorstep-thick bread with lashings of melting butter. My love of pork has since grown from a passion to an obsession!

Over the twenty-plus years I've worked as a chef in kitchens across the globe, I've always felt that pork has been given the "cheap seat" on menus, and maybe hasn't been treated with the same respect as other types of meat. I wanted to change this and so I opened a restaurant in the heart of the City of London and called it *The English Pig*. For me, pork has so much to offer and now's the time to show the pig in all its glory...

Pork is now often called "the other white meat" as breeders produce cuts that are leaner and healthier, but the most fantastic thing about pork is its versatility – it provides lean cuts, fattier cuts and cuts for roasting, stewing or braising. Cured, smoked and air-dried pork has become a culinary art in its own right and has led to some of the most sought-after delicacies in the world, such as Iberico, Serrano, Parma and Bellota hams, as well as spectacular sausages and salami. Pound for pound, the pig is amazing.

With today's modern approach to pig farming, unfortunately there are still varying standards of animal welfare. Though I'm always pleased to discover that there are still a number of amazing farmers who believe in their product, and finding them is of utmost importance to me. I visit farms at least half a dozen times a year, checking on quality control and whether these wonderful omnivores are being looked after in the right way.

I take sourcing very seriously and my preference is for outdoor-reared pork, as this allows the pig to follow its natural instincts of foraging and burrowing for its own food. A natural and varied diet is crucial to the flavour of pork, and the pig needs to eat almost constantly. This explains its quick growth: at around nine months old the pig has reached its optimum meat-to-bone ratio. Outdoor rearing allows for socializing and this is a very important trait when making sure the animal is happy within its environment and itself. A calm pig is a happy pig, and a happy pig produces the most amazing meat!

BREEDS OF PIG

There are hundreds, if not thousands, of breeds of pig across the globe, with some breeds reared for their fresh meat and others more suited to cured ham.

Of the fourteen rare breeds I love to cook with, my favourite is the Gloucester Old Spot [1] because the beautiful layers of fat on the belly make it the perfect piece for slow cooking. I also look for Saddlebacks [2], which are longer in the body, resulting in stunning loins and tenderloins (fillet). Sandy and Black, Tamworth and British Lop [3] are also worth looking out for due to their great flavour and lean meat content.

In certain parts of Europe, particularly in hilly regions, certain breeds have been chosen for their suitability for ham. All that hill climbing (and acorn eating) gives a wonderful texture and taste to the haunch of the pig. The much-coveted and DOC-protected (*Denominación de Origen*) dry-cured Spanish hams – Iberico, Bellota and jamon Serrano – are some of the most revered. Iberico Black pigs [4] are pure or cross bred with other breeds and mainly come from southern Spain. Bellota is from free-range pigs that roam the Iberian peninsula, and whose diet is made up almost entirely of acorns, while Serrano comes mainly from Landrace pigs, but also from Duroc [5] and Pietrain.

Italian prosciutto di Parma and San Daniele are also fine-quality, popular hams and they usually come from the Large White, Landrace or Duroc pigs. The Tuscan equivalent is the La Cinta Senese or Sienese Banded pig, which is sought after for prosciutto.

Across Eastern and Central Europe, one of the most popular breeds is the Krskopolje, or Blackbelted Pig, which is celebrated for its large size and quality of meat. The Mangalitsa [6] is very popular in Hungary, especially as it has a great fat content with beautiful marbling, making it fantastic for hams and salami. In Germany, the Swabian-Hall is a rare breed that is revered for its fattier flesh and has a geographical status protected by the European Union.

North American breeds are relatively new and mainly bred for their lean meat. The Duroc is probably the most "traditional" and was bred initially in the states of New York and New Jersey in the 1800s. The breed is unique due to its bright auburn skin.

COOKING WITH PORK

Our mothers were most likely taught to cook pork thoroughly, which often made it quite dry, but now, due to new standards in pig farming, better guidelines on feed and improvements in transport, you really can eat pork slightly pink! Even the US Department of Agriculture has fully embraced this trend. In 2011, it reduced the recommended internal temperature for cooked pork from 74°C/165°F (thoroughly cooked and possibly dry) to 63°C/145°F, when it is slightly rosy and still moist.

When cooking with pork, certain cuts suit some dishes better than others. Broadly speaking, the parts of a pig that do a lot of work, such as the legs and cheeks, are muscular and tougher, so need long slow-cooking. Those that do little, such as the tenderloin fillet and loin, are lean and benefit from quick cooking. To make things easy, my suggestions for using each cut of pork will help you to cook this wonderful meat perfectly.

Cooking with pork loin

The loin of a pig is one of the most versatile cuts of pork and it is also one of the most expensive. As with other animals, the muscles in the loin area do very little work and so the meat tends to be lean, and it also has a more subtle flavour than the shoulder or the legs.

A loin joint is one of the most popular roasting cuts and although the meat is fairly lean, it has a good outer layer of fat and skin, which keeps the meat moist and makes fantastic crispy crackling. Conventional roasting at a higher temperature is ideal for pork loin, although it can be oven cooked more gently, if required (see Pork Loin in a Fennel Salt Crust, page 172). A boneless loin roast is easy to carve and can also be opened out and filled with a stuffing for extra flavour and moisture (see Rolled Loin of Pork with Ricotta & Basil, page 70). Meat roasted on the bone is usually seen as the ultimate way to impart flavour, and a loin rack joint is very manageable for the home cook. If you are concerned about carving, ask your butcher to cut the meat away from the bones, then tie it back on. The meat can be easily lifted away from the bones for carving after roasting.

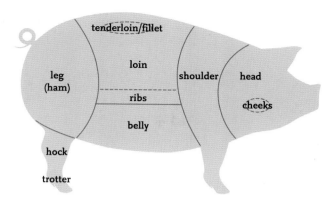

The fillet, also known as the tenderloin, comes from within the loin area and it is very lean and tender [*pictured overleaf, left*]. It is a long, thin, cyclindrical cut, around 6–8cm/2½–3½in in diameter with very little fat, though the tenderloin does have a covering of pale white silvery membrane. This is called the silverskin, a type of connective tissue that doesn't break down when cooked. It can be tough, so it is best removed with a sharp knife before cooking. (See "Show Me How" to Prepare and Cook the Tenderloin, page 68.) The lean fillet is best cooked quickly and left slightly pink in the centre so that it stays moist and juicy. The shape of the fillet makes it ideal for cutting into thin slices or thicker medallions and pan frying (see Pork Medallions with Brandy-soaked Prunes, page 67). The fillet also takes strong flavours well, and is particularly good marinated before cooking (see Korean-style Fiery Pork, page 130). It can be wrapped in bacon and roasted briefly (see Pancetta-wrapped Pork with Mushroom Stuffing, page 110) or pan-fried whole (see Coriander-crusted Pork, page 132).

Loin chops and steaks are great for quick and easy weeknight meals. Chops have both bone and fat to help provide flavour and moisture and can be quickly pan fried, griddled or grilled (see Grilled Garlic & Sage Pork Chops, page 53). Loin steaks don't have bones and may come with or without fat but are fantastic for beating into thin escalopes for super-quick cooking (see Pork Saltimbocca, page 109), or cut into thin strips or pieces for stir fries (see Sweet & Sour Pork, page 59).

Baby back ribs also come from the loin area of pork. These ribs are always best done in a whole rack, barbecue-style, low and slow (see Sticky Barbecue Ribs, page 168).

Cooking with pork leg

Pork leg from the hindquarters of the pig (usually sold fresh or as ham) is heavily muscled and consequently much leaner than the shoulder and belly. Sadly, this part of the pig has probably contributed most to the belief that pork can be dry, as it needs more careful cooking than some other cuts. Maybe then it is no surprise that legs are most commonly cured as ham.

Legs can be sold on or off the bone, but due to the size of the joint it is usually available boneless and cut into portions. If it is on the bone, try to choose a piece from the lower, or shank, end of the leg as it is a more manageable size and easier to carve.

Pot-roasting is one of the best ways to cook pork leg (see Pot-roasted Leg of Pork with Sweet Garlic, page 193). This method creates a slightly steamy environment to keep the meat moist during cooking. The leg can also be marinated overnight in oil and herbs for extra flavour. Pork leg comes into its own in slow-cooked curries and stews (see Pork Goulash, page 194), because even after long cooking the meat tends to hold together.

The leg can be conventionally roasted, but its lower fat content means that it is not the best cut for slow roasting. If you want to roast a leg joint and keep it moist, then you could "lard" the meat by threading strips of pork fat through the joint using a special larding needle, which you can buy from kitchen shops or online. Alternatively, if it is a boneless rolled joint then you could stuff it, re-roll and tie with string. Weigh the stuffed joint and calculate the cooking time as 45 minutes per kg/20 minutes per lb, plus an extra 30 minutes. Preheat the oven to 225°C/ 425°F/Gas 7 and roast the leg for 30 minutes to crisp the skin, then reduce the temperature to 180°C/350°F/Gas 4 for the remaining time. Like most meat, a roasted leg needs to rest after cooking.

Leg steaks can be quite dry, so they should be marinated and then cooked very quickly and left a little pink. Since the muscle fibres in the leg are quite long, it can be useful to tenderize the meat by beating it with a meat mallet or rolling pin before cooking. The meat can also be cut across the grain into thin strips to use for stir-frying.

Ham can be bought on or off the bone, and again for most home-cooks a boneless ham is a more manageable option. It can be smoked or unsmoked, and since most ham today tends to be mild-cured, it will probably not need soaking before cooking. If you are not sure about its saltiness, then test it by following my tip on Home-cooked Ham in Ginger & Mustard Glaze (see page 210). Uncooked ham is best simmered in water rather than roasted, because this is a more gentle form of cooking. However, you can roast a larger on-the-bone ham if soaked overnight, drained, then wrapped in a foil parcel. Preheat the oven to 160°C/325°F/Gas 3 and cook for 45 minutes per kg/20 minutes per lb, followed by glazing and baking at a higher temperature for a golden, glossy coating.

Cooking with pork shoulder

If you look at a cut from a pork shoulder, you are likely to notice that there is a fair amount of fat marbling through the meat or muscle, which makes it very flavourful and also ideal for slow-cooking, because the meat remains moist while the fat melts away. The structure of the meat also means that it tends to fall apart once it has been cooked.

The shoulder covers quite a large area of the pig and it is commonly sold as the collar, which is the top neck end of the shoulder, or the blade, the upper part of the shoulder. These cuts can be sold boneless or on the bone.

Shoulder joints with their skin on are perfect for slow roasting (see Eight-hour Roast Shoulder of Pork, page 170). Make sure you score the skin first as it will crisp up as the fat renders away, producing delicious crackling. You need a blast of high heat, preferably at the beginning of roasting, for successful crackling. The high heat will also help to colour the outside of the meat and leave caramelized bits (called the *fond*) on the bottom and sides of the roasting tin, which you can then use to make a flavoursome gravy.

Shoulder cuts are good for barbecuing very slowly over wood chips. Again, the fat content will help to keep the meat moist and also the cooked pork is easy to shred, or pull apart, with two forks, making it ideal for pulled pork.

Shoulder cuts are also sold as pork steaks. The meat from this cut can be on the tough side, so shoulder steaks should be cooked very quickly and left slightly pink. Pan-frying is the best method for this; make sure the pan is very hot before the meat is added and the steaks can be flavoured with a rub of herby or spicy salt before cooking. If the shoulder is cubed and stewed, then it tends to break down into shreds, making it perfect for ragus or meat-based sauces.

The very bottom part of the shoulder, extending down to the leg, is known as the knuckle or hock; this is the "elbow" section before you reach the trotter. The knuckle can be cured to make ham hocks or left uncured, but either way it needs very long, slow cooking until the meat literally falls away from the bone. A ham hock needs to be covered in liquid and then simmered as the curing process can leave the meat a little dry if it is braised or roasted, although like other hams it can be finished in the oven. The best way to cook an uncured knuckle is to braise it in a little liquid to keep it moist, then finish with a period of high heat to crisp the skin on the outside (see Braised Pork Knuckle in Cider, page 206).

Cooking with pork belly

If there was ever a piece of meat that has gone from cheap cut to culinary superstar then it would have to be pork belly. The fatty underside of the pig used to be routinely overlooked

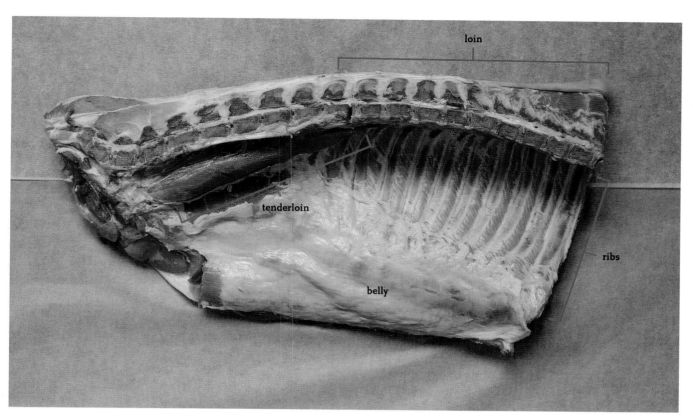

loin

tenderloin

belly

ribs

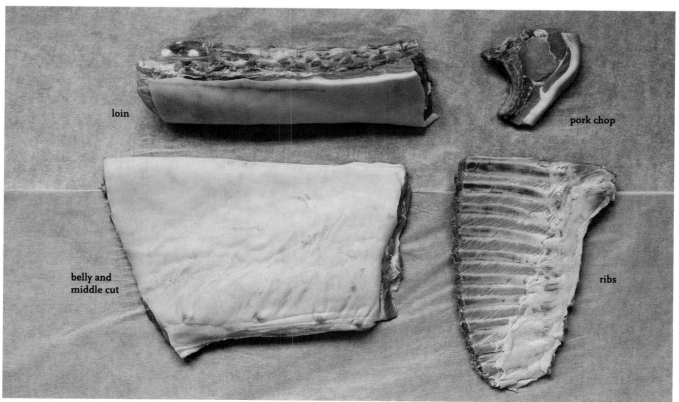

loin

pork chop

belly and
middle cut

ribs

by home cooks, but in more recent years its true value has been recognized. When cooked, the layers of skin, flesh and fat give an optimal mix of crisp, crackling shards of skin and flavoursome tender meat. The belly has now been firmly embraced by cooks in the West, but it may come as no surprise to find that the Asians have revered this cut for some time. Not only does pork belly taste great, it's also pretty versatile: it can be preserved (see Confit of Pork Belly, page 181, and How to Cure Bacon, page 98); braised (see Japanese Pork Belly, page 192) or roasted (see Slow-roasted Pork Belly, page 189).

Pork belly is made up of a layer of skin, a subcutaneous layer of fat, a layer of muscle, a second layer of fat plus connective tissue and a second layer of muscle. This lamination of fat and meat gives the belly its fantastic flavour and also plenty of moisture, which means that slow-roasting is perhaps the best way of all to cook it. An initial blast of high heat in the oven will start to blister and crisp the scored skin, but after this the oven needs to be turned down to low to allow the fat to melt slowly away. During roasting it needs very little attention. To prevent the pork sitting in a pool of grease while it roasts, it's best to sit the belly on a trivet made of vegetables, or on a metal rack, so that the rendered fat slides away into the bottom of the tin.

Since the belly retains a lot of moisture during cooking, it is an ideal cut to cook ahead. First braise the belly in an aromatic stock, then leave to cool and put it in the fridge until ready to serve. Before serving, portion the meat and reheat it fairly quickly in a hot pan or oven – this is one restaurant trick that works well in a home kitchen. The gelatine from the meat will enrich the braising liquid and it can be reduced down to make a delicious accompanying sauce or gravy, once the fat has been skimmed away (see Chinese Pork Belly with Seasoned Rice, page 186).

One of the ways I like to cook pork belly in my restaurants is to braise it for 16 hours with carrots and onions until it is so tender that the meat literally falls apart. The pork is then shredded, keeping the paler upper layer and the darker lower layers separate, and pressed in alternate layers with the braised vegetables. Finally, it is cut into squares, breadcrumbed and fried, and served cut into wedges. It is the ultimate pork "sandwich"!

Cooking with the rest of the pig

There is a popular saying about the pig that "you can eat everything but the squeal". In recent years there has been a revival in the popularity of nose-to-tail eating, and cuts like trotters have started to appear again on restaurant menus and even in some supermarkets.

There are many classic dishes that celebrate the trotter, such as *crubeens* from Ireland, *pied de cochon* from France, and the spicy Korean *jokbal*. Pickled pigs' trotters are also popular in many cuisines. The one thing that these recipes all have in common, however, is the initial long, slow cooking. One of the wonderful by-products of this technique is that you will end up with a stock rich in gelatine, which is ideal for pies and terrines. The remaining trotter can then be cooked in many ways: stuffed, baked, coated in breadcrumbs, or cooked in a rich sauce and served in slices. As an added benefit, some people believe that eating the collagen in the trotter keeps you looking young!

A pig's head is also very versatile, but often ends up as a terrine known, rather unglamourously, as brawn or head cheese. The head is usually soaked in brine first, then slowly poached in a spiced stock until the meat can be pulled away from the bones and shredded. Often trotters are added to increase the meat content and for a richer stock. The meat is packed into a terrine or bowl and covered with the strained stock, which forms a jelly when chilled. The brawn is served sliced, usually with toast and a salad.

A pig's cheek, however, is by far and away the hidden treasure. All animal cheeks do a lot of work and are therefore fairly tough, but when cooked slowly they become amazingly tender and again the collagen in the meat oozes out to deliver an incredibly rich sauce. As a pig's cheek is fairly small, you will need two per person, but the size is also an advantage as it means it cooks more quickly than some of the larger cuts. If you were going to try any of the more unusual cuts of pork, I would urge you to try this one (see Pork Cheeks with Caramelized Fennel, page 204).

While it is true that you can't make a silk purse out of a sow's ear, you can turn this part of the pig into a tasty treat. The ear is mainly fat and cartilage and is really best cooked until crisp (see Crispy Pigs' Ears, page 165). The crisp morsels can be served as a snack or appetizer, or even as a crunchy garnish to a salad. However, a word of warning: the ear retains a lot of liquid so it tends to spit when it hits the hot fat.

Now to the tail… although perceived as a skinny part of the anatomy, the tail does contain some meat and a good amount of fat. It is particularly popular in the Caribbean and some of the southern states of America. It can be stewed, but is most popular braised until tender, then roasted or barbecued until crisp.

PRESERVED PORK

Most popular methods of pork preservation have been around for thousands of years. Pigs were traditionally slaughtered in the late autumn, partly because it was expensive and impractical to feed animals during the winter and partly because they would have been fattened during the warmer months on windfalls, nuts and seeds. Charcuterie, which comes from the French words *chair*, meaning "flesh", and *cuite*, meaning "cooked", was developed to improve the keeping qualities of meat during the cooler winter months.

Pretty much all pork preservation starts with curing: treating the meat with salt, either mixed with water to make a brine, or by applying a dry salt mixture to the surface of the meat. The salt draws out moisture from the meat, which is vital for preservation because bacteria needs moisture to grow. Salt also slows down the fermentation process that breaks down the meat fibres, keeping the meat firm. Alongside salt, saltpetre and, more recently, sodium nitrate, or nitrite, is added to help stop the meat going off and to prevent bacteria formation.

Bacon and ham are probably the most popular types of preserved pork. They are made in a similar manner with ham being cured for longer than bacon (see How to Cure Bacon, page 98). In many countries, ham is air-dried after curing and matured to further preserve it and enhance its flavour, such as prosciutto di Parma, Iberico and jamon Serrano. Prosciutto takes between 9 months and 2 years before it is ready to be eaten. Ham and bacon can also be smoked for additional flavour, although smoking in itself does not preserve pork. Ham and bacon are usually hung in a smokehouse and cold smoked for up to 2 days. Pork can also be almost completely dried to make jerky, which is popular in South Africa.

Salame, or *saucisson sec*, is a sausage that is cured and air dried to preserve it. Usually a mixture of pork shoulder and fat is finely chopped or minced and mixed with a curing salt mixture before being stuffed into a sausage casing. Salame differs from ham in that it is fermented first, often by adding acidophilus, a type of "friendly" bacteria. It is perfectly safe and often seen as the dry white bloom on the outside of an artisanal salame. The salame is then air-dried for several weeks and often a white mould is applied to the casing to reduce exposure to air and improve its keeping qualities. It is possible to make salame at home, although it is advisable to test its pH balance after the initial fermentation to make sure it is safe to eat. You will also need to have a cool place with good air circulation for drying the sausages.

Preserving in fat is also a popular way to keep pork (see Goose Fat Potted Pork, page 76). French rillettes, for example, is one of the earliest types of pâté and is made by slowly cooking pork in pork fat until very tender. The pork is then shredded, packed into sterilized jars and covered with the fat. Confit pork is in a similar vein, although cooked in goose or duck fat, rather than pork fat, and usually left in larger pieces (see Confit of Pork Belly, page 181).

CHOOSING PORK

Good meat comes from good farming. A happy pig is more likely to give soft, succulent flesh than one that has been raised in a stressful environment. The flavour of the meat can also be influenced by the pig's diet, with a varied and natural diet more likely to give tastier meat than a bland, monotonous one. While rearing standards have improved enormously over the years, in some places they are still not perfect, so it is very important to try and buy from shops who know the source or provenance of their meat. A local butcher is usually a great place to buy, but this is often not practical for many people. However, there are some supermarket chains that only buy from reliable sources and can trace the origins of

5–6 rashers thick-cut, smoked streaky bacon
2 tbsp maple syrup
4 tbsp extra virgin olive oil
2 tbsp good-quality balsamic vinegar
200g/7oz baby spinach leaves

1 large nectarine, pitted and thinly sliced
75g/2^{1}/$_{2}$oz/^{3}/$_{4}$ cup pecan halves, roughly broken
1 fresh red chilli, deseeded and thinly sliced
salt and freshly ground black pepper
crusty bread, to serve

SERVES 4 | **PREPARATION TIME** 15 minutes | **COOKING TIME** 15 minutes

BACON & NECTARINE SALAD

The contrast of the crisp salty bacon with the sweet maple syrup makes your taste buds dance with delight!

1] Preheat the oven to 200°C/400°F/Gas 6. Lay the bacon in a single layer on a wire rack set over a roasting tin, lined with foil. Roast for about 10 minutes, then brush both sides of the rashers with the maple syrup and cook for a further 2–3 minutes until golden and slightly crisp. Remove the bacon from the oven and leave it to cool for 2 minutes as the maple glaze will be very hot, then break into bite-sized pieces.

2] Whisk together the oil and vinegar, then season with salt and pepper. Put the spinach in a large serving bowl and toss with most of the dressing. Add the nectarine and bacon and gently mix in. Scatter the pecans and chilli over the top. Drizzle the remaining dressing over the salad and serve immediately with slices of crusty bread.

JOHNNIE'S TIP

Roasting bacon on a rack in the oven is a great way to cook it for a large number of people. You can also flavour the bacon with other ingredients such as paprika, honey or even a little apricot jam that has been thinned with a small amount of water to make it more spreadable.

"SHOW ME HOW" TO ROAST THE BACON

300g/10½oz small waxy potatoes, such as
   Ratte, Anya or Pink Fir Apple
4 large eggs
200g/7oz lardons, cubetti di pancetta or diced
   smoked streaky bacon
olive oil, as needed

1 tbsp red wine vinegar or sherry vinegar
½ tsp sugar, or to taste
1 head of frisée lettuce, pale inner
   leaves only, torn
freshly ground black pepper
baguette or crusty bread, to serve

SERVES 4 | **PREPARATION TIME** 15 minutes | **COOKING TIME** 35 minutes

EGG, BACON & POTATO SALAD

Runny egg, crispy bacon and bittersweet frisée make a perfect combination.

1] Put the potatoes in a large saucepan of cold salted water over a high heat. Bring to the boil, then turn the heat down and cook for 12–15 minutes until tender. Drain and leave to one side to cool slightly, then break or cut into bite-sized slices.

2] Meanwhile, put the eggs in a large saucepan and add enough cold water to cover by 1cm/½in. Bring to the boil over a medium heat, then remove the pan from the heat and leave to stand for 12 minutes. Drain the eggs and cool under cold running water, giving them a little tap to crack the shells. When the eggs are cool, peel and halve them.

3] To desalt the lardons, put them in a medium-sized saucepan and just cover with water. Bring up to simmering point, then drain and repeat this process. Drain again and pat dry with kitchen paper. Put the lardons in a large dry frying pan over a low heat. Cook for 8–10 minutes, turning occasionally, until the fat seeps out of the lardons, then turn the heat up to medium and fry for 3–4 minutes until golden and crisp. Put a sieve over a measuring jug and tip the lardons into the sieve, letting the fat drip into the jug.

4] Add enough olive oil to the lardon fat to make 60ml/2fl oz/¼ cup, then whisk in the vinegar and sugar to make a dressing. Season with pepper (you are unlikely to need salt as the lardons are quite salty), taste and add more sugar if the dressing is too sharp.

5] Mix the potatoes, frisée, lardons and eggs gently together in a bowl and drizzle the dressing over the top. Serve with slices of baguette or crusty bread.

"SHOW ME HOW" TO DESALT THE LARDONS

300g/10½oz/1½ cups dried split green peas, rinsed

1 smoked ham hock, about 750g/1lb 10oz total weight

2 large onions, 1 quartered and the other finely chopped

2 large carrots, 1 scrubbed and halved and the other finely diced

6 black peppercorns

1 bay leaf

125g/4½oz unsalted butter

1 large leek, finely chopped

2 celery stalks, finely diced

1.5l/52fl oz/6 cups vegetable stock

1 bouquet garni

salt and freshly ground black pepper

crusty bread, to serve

SERVES 4 | PREPARATION TIME 15 minutes, plus overnight soaking | COOKING TIME 4 hours

HAM, LEEK & PEA SOUP

Classic pea and ham soup doesn't look that great, but the flavour is amazing. This is an old family recipe passed down through many generations of Mountains!

1] Put the peas in a large bowl. Cover with cold water and leave to soak overnight.

2] Put the ham hock in a large saucepan and cover with cold water. Add the quartered onion, halved carrot, peppercorns and bay leaf. Bring the water to the boil over a high heat, then turn the heat down to low and simmer, part-covered, for 2 hours. Drain the ham, reserving 250ml/9fl oz/1 cup of the cooking stock, and discard the remainder with the cooked vegetables.

3] Meanwhile, drain the peas, rinse and drain again. Leave to one side.

4] Melt the butter in a second large saucepan over a low heat. Add the remaining onion and carrot as well as the leek and celery. Cook for about 15 minutes, stirring occasionally, until softened but not coloured. Add the drained peas, vegetable stock and bouquet garni. Transfer the ham hock to the pan. Bring the stock to the boil, then turn the heat down and simmer, part-covered, for 1–1½ hours until the peas start to disintegrate and the ham is coming away from the bone.

5] Remove the ham from the pan and pull away the meat, tearing it into bite-sized chunks. Discard any skin, fat and bone. Remove the bouquet garni and season with salt and pepper, to taste. (You can purée the soup using a hand blender at this stage if you prefer it smooth, adding some of the ham cooking liquid if it is too thick.)

6] Return the ham to the soup, stir, and warm gently over a low heat before serving with crusty bread.

225g/8oz/scant 1³/₄ cups strong white flour,
plus extra for dusting
7g/¹/₄oz easy-blend yeast
¹/₂ tsp salt, plus extra to taste
¹/₂ tsp sugar
3 tbsp olive oil, plus extra for greasing
50g/1³/₄oz pancetta or smoked streaky bacon

4 large onions, thinly sliced
4 thyme sprigs
15 black olives, pitted and halved
freshly ground black pepper
green salad, to serve

SERVES 4–6 | **PREPARATION TIME** 1¹/₂ hours, including rising | **COOKING TIME** 30 minutes

PROVENÇAL BACON & ONION TART

The sweet onions are offset by a salty kick in this popular French onion tart, but here the saltiness comes from the pancetta, rather than the usual anchovies.

1] Mix together the flour, yeast, salt and sugar in a large bowl. Make a well in the centre and add 1 tablespoon of the olive oil, plus 125ml/4fl oz/¹/₂ cup hand-hot water. Mix together, adding more water as needed to make a soft dough. Turn the dough out onto a lightly floured work surface and knead for about 10 minutes until smooth and springy. Lightly grease a clean bowl with a little olive oil. Put the dough in the bowl, cover with cling film, and leave to rise in a warm place for 1 hour or until doubled in size.

2] Meanwhile, cook the pancetta in a large dry, non-stick frying pan over a medium heat for 6 minutes, turning once, until crisp. Remove from the pan, then leave to cool slightly. Break the pancetta into pieces and set aside on a plate lined with kitchen paper.

3] Add the onions to the pan along with the remaining 2 tablespoons olive oil, 2 tablespoons water and the thyme. Cover the pan and turn the heat down to low. Cook the onions for about 40 minutes, stirring regularly, until very soft. Remove the lid, increase the heat to medium, then cook for a further 5–10 minutes to remove any excess moisture. Season the onions with salt and pepper, remove the thyme sprigs and leave the onions to one side.

4] Preheat the oven to 200°C/400°F/Gas 6. Lightly oil the base but not the sides of a large baking tray.

5] Turn the dough onto the baking tray and press it out to cover the base and up the sides. Spread the onions in an even layer over the dough and top with the olives and pancetta pieces. Bake for 25–30 minutes until the base of the dough is golden and crisp. Leave the tart to cool slightly, then serve with a green salad.

325g/11½oz/2⅔ cups plain flour, plus extra
  for dusting
½ tsp salt
2 eggs, lightly beaten
40g/1½oz unsalted butter
70g/2½oz lard
pickle or chutney, to serve

JELLY
1 ham bone or 200g/7oz pork bones
1 onion, quartered
1 carrot, scrubbed and cut into 5cm/2in pieces
1 celery stalk, cut in half
1 bay leaf
4 black peppercorns
1 gelatine leaf (2g)

FILLING
200g/7oz pork shoulder, cubed
3 slices streaky bacon, about 50g/1¾oz
  total weight
3 large sage leaves, finely chopped
4 dried apricots, finely chopped
⅛ tsp ground allspice
freshly grated nutmeg
vegetable oil, for frying and greasing
salt and freshly ground black pepper

MAKES 8 | PREPARATION TIME 2 hours, plus initial cooling & overnight chilling |
COOKING TIME 45 minutes

PORK PIES [pictured overleaf]

True satisfaction is producing your own pork pie! Don't be scared of attempting the hot-water crust, because the pastry really is straightforward to make.

1] To make the pastry, sift the flour and salt into a large bowl and stir in one of the eggs. Melt the butter and lard in a small saucepan with 150ml/5fl oz/scant ⅔ cup cold water over a low heat. Turn the heat up and bring the mixture to the boil, then immediately remove the pan from the heat. Stir the hot fat into the flour, mixing with a wooden spoon until it forms a thick paste. Put the paste on a large piece of cling film and pat into a disc, then wrap and put it in the fridge for 1 hour.

2] Meanwhile, to make the jelly, put the ham bone, onion, carrot and celery in a medium-sized saucepan and add 1 litre/35fl oz/4 cups water. Bring to the boil over a medium heat, skimming off any foamy scum that rises to the surface of the water, then turn the heat down to low. Add the bay leaf and peppercorns and simmer very gently for 1 hour.

3] To make the filling, finely chop the pork and bacon by hand or in a food processor (use pulse so that the meat isn't too finely minced). Put the meat in a bowl and stir in the sage, apricots and allspice, plus several gratings of nutmeg. [continued on page 37]

Season with salt and pepper. Fry 1 teaspoon of the mixture, then taste, adding more allspice, nutmeg, salt and pepper, if required. The filling will taste milder when cold, so you can be generous with the seasoning.

4] Preheat the oven to 180°C/350°F/Gas 4. Roll out two-thirds of the pastry on a lightly floured surface until 3mm/⅛in thick. Using a 9cm/3½in round cutter, press out 8 circles. Lightly grease 8 cups of a muffin tin and put a circle of pastry in each. Press the pastry into the bottom and up the side of each cup, leaving a slight overhang. Put 2 tablespoonfuls of the filling into each pastry case.

5] Roll out the remaining pastry to 2mm/¹⁄₁₆in thick and cut out 8 more circles using a 7cm/2¾in cutter. Brush the edge of each pie with some of the remaining beaten egg and put the pastry circle tops on, crimping the edges with a small fork. Decorate with the pastry trimmings, if you like. Glaze the pies with the remaining beaten egg, then cut a steam hole in the top of each pie (make sure it is fairly open). Bake for 30 minutes until the pastry is golden brown. Cool slightly in the tin, then use a table knife to ease out the pies and cool on a wire rack for 1 hour.

6] Meanwhile, strain the ham bone cooking liquid into a clean saucepan, discarding the bone and vegetables. Bring to the boil over a high heat, then turn the heat down and simmer until reduced to 100ml/3½fl oz/scant ½ cup. Remove from the heat and season with salt and pepper. Soak the gelatine leaf in cold water for 5 minutes until soft and pliable, then squeeze it out and whisk into the hot liquid until dissolved. Using a pipette or spoon, carefully add a little of the liquid into each pie through the steam hole – you should just see the liquid covering the surface of the cooked pork. Leave to cool.

7] Put the pork pies in the fridge overnight to allow the jelly to set and the flavours to develop slightly before serving with a spoonful of pickle or chutney.

JOHNNIE'S TIP

To make the jelly mixture from scratch, without the use of gelatine, add a pig's trotter to the pan with the ham bone or pork bones and pour in enough water to just cover. Bring to the boil, then turn the heat down and simmer for 1 hour. Strain the liquid and reduce as in Step 6, above. Leave the liquid to stand in a cool place for 1 hour and skim off as much fat from the surface as possible. Warm gently before spooning it into the pies.

250g/9oz/2 cups plain flour
½ tsp salt, plus extra to taste
5 eggs
300ml/10½fl oz/scant 1¼ cups milk
6 tbsp vegetable oil
8 good-quality sausages, about 450g/1lb total weight
peas or other green vegetable, to serve

ONION GRAVY
30g/1oz unsalted butter
2 large red onions, thinly sliced
1 small thyme sprig, leaves finely chopped
1 tsp plain flour
60ml/2fl oz/¼ cup red wine
300ml/10½fl oz/scant 1¼ cups beef stock
1–2 tsp redcurrant jelly
freshly ground black pepper

SERVES 4 | **PREPARATION TIME** 20 minutes | **COOKING TIME** 1 hour 10 minutes

TOAD IN THE HOLE WITH ONION GRAVY

1] To make the batter, sift the flour and salt into a bowl. Whisk the eggs and milk with 4 tablespoons water, then gradually whisk three-quarters of the mixture into the flour to make a smooth batter. Whisk in the remaining milk mixture, a little at a time, until the consistency of single cream. Transfer to a jug and leave to rest until ready to use.

2] To make the gravy, melt the butter in a large frying pan over a medium heat. When the butter is foaming, add the onions and thyme. Turn the heat down slightly, cover the pan, and cook the onions for 30 minutes, stirring frequently, until soft. Uncover the pan, increase the heat to medium and cook for a further 10 minutes until the onions have slightly caramelized. Stir in the flour, then whisk in the red wine and stock. Bring to the boil, then turn the heat down and simmer for 10–15 minutes until the gravy has thickened slightly. Whisk in 1 teaspoon of the redcurrant jelly, adding more to taste, if you like. Season with salt and pepper and leave to one side.

3] While the onions are cooking, preheat the oven to 220°C/425°F/Gas 7.

4] Heat 2 tablespoons of the oil in a large frying pan over a medium heat. Add the sausages and cook for 8–10 minutes, turning them regularly, until golden brown all over. It is important to brown them properly as they won't colour in the batter. While the sausages are cooking, pour the remaining oil in a medium-sized roasting tin and heat in the oven for 5 minutes until very hot.

5] Carefully remove the tin from the oven and put it on the hob over a medium heat. Pour in the batter (it should start to bubble at the edges) and sit the sausages in the batter. Immediately return the tin to the oven and bake for 10 minutes. Turn the heat down to 200°C/400°F/Gas 6 and bake for a further 25–30 minutes until the batter is puffy on top and crisp on the bottom. Reheat the gravy, if necessary, and serve with the "toad". I like to serve this with peas, but any green vegetable would be great.

1 tbsp olive oil

1 onion, finely chopped

1 garlic clove, crushed

2 small thyme sprigs, leaves finely chopped

1/2 recipe quantity Passata (see page 212), about 750ml/26fl oz/3 cups

500g/1lb 2oz lean pork mince

1 handful of flat-leaf parsley leaves, finely chopped

30g/1oz Grana Padano or Parmesan cheese, finely grated, plus extra to serve

2 pinches of ground nutmeg

400g/14oz dried linguine

100g/3½oz mozzarella cheese, drained and grated

salt and freshly ground black pepper

green salad, to serve

SERVES 4 | PREPARATION TIME 20 minutes, not including the passata | COOKING TIME 1 hour

PORK MEATBALLS WITH LINGUINE

Better than "mamma used to make" – this is the perfect light lunch.

1] Preheat the oven to 180°C/350°F/Gas 4. Heat the oil in a large frying pan over a low heat. Fry the onion for 8–10 minutes until soft and translucent. Add the garlic and thyme and cook for a further 1 minute. Transfer to a large bowl and leave to cool.

2] Warm the passata in a medium-sized saucepan. Season with salt and pepper.

3] Meanwhile, add the pork, parsley and Grana Padano to the cooked onion mixture. Mix together and season with nutmeg, salt and pepper. (You can check the seasoning by frying a teaspoonful of the pork mixture in a small frying pan.)

4] Form tablespoonfuls of the mixture into meatballs and put them into a medium-sized ovenproof dish. Pour the warm passata over and cover tightly with foil. Bake for 40–45 minutes until the sauce is bubbling and the meatballs are cooked through.

5] Cook the linguine in a large saucepan of boiling salted water for 12 minutes or until al dente, then drain. Remove the dish from the oven, uncover, add the drained pasta and gently toss everything together. Scatter the mozzarella over the top.

6] Heat the grill to high and grill for 2–3 minutes until the mozzarella has melted. Serve with extra Grana Padano and a green salad.

JOHNNIE'S TIP

The pork mixture makes fairly firm meatballs, so if you prefer slightly softer ones, soak 2 slices of crustless white bread in 4 tablespoons milk for 10 minutes, then squeeze out the excess liquid. Tear the bread into small pieces and put it into the bowl with the onion mixture before adding the mince.

200g/7oz/1¼ cups dried macaroni
75g/2½oz pancetta, cut into bite-sized pieces
40g/1½oz unsalted butter
40g/1½oz/⅓ cup plain flour
750ml/26fl oz/3 cups milk
1 heaped tsp Dijon mustard
125g/4½oz Gruyère cheese, grated

40g/1½oz Parmesan cheese, finely grated
cayenne pepper, to taste
2 tbsp fresh white breadcrumbs (from
 ½ slice of bread)
salt and ground white pepper
crisp green salad, to serve

SERVES 4 | **PREPARATION TIME** 20 minutes | **COOKING TIME** 40 minutes

PANCETTA MAC & CHEESE

Macaroni cheese is an all-time favourite comfort food, and this version has an extra layer of taste with the addition of crispy bites of smoky pancetta.

1] Preheat the oven to 220°C/425°F/Gas 7. Cook the macaroni in a large saucepan of boiling salted water for 10–12 minutes until al dente. Drain and rinse under cold running water, then leave to one side to drain.

2] Meanwhile, put the pancetta in a large, dry frying pan over a low heat. Cook for 4–5 minutes, turning once, until the fat has run out of the pancetta. Increase the heat to medium and cook until crisp. Transfer the pancetta to a plate lined with kitchen paper.

3] Melt the butter in a large saucepan over a low heat and stir in the flour to make a paste. Take the pan off the heat and whisk in the milk, a little at a time, to make a smooth sauce. Return to the heat and cook, stirring constantly, until the sauce comes to the boil and thickens slightly. Turn the heat down and simmer for 1 minute, stirring.

4] Remove the pan from the heat and stir in the mustard, Gruyère and Parmesan, reserving 2 tablespoons. Season to taste with cayenne, salt and pepper. Add the pancetta and cooked macaroni to the pan and turn until combined. Check the seasoning.

5] Tip the pasta and sauce into an ovenproof dish and place on a baking sheet. Mix together the breadcrumbs and the reserved Parmesan and scatter the mixture over the pasta. Bake for 20 minutes until the top is golden and the sauce is bubbling. Serve with a crisp green salad.

100g/3½oz Parma ham
400g/14oz dried spaghetti
4 egg yolks
100g/3½oz Parmesan cheese, finely grated,
  plus extra to serve

1 tsp olive oil
125g/4½oz unsalted butter, cut into
  small cubes
1 tbsp finely chopped flat-leaf parsley leaves
salt and freshly grated black pepper

SERVES 4 | **PREPARATION TIME** 10 minutes | **COOKING TIME** 12 minutes

PARMA HAM CARBONARA

Spaghetti carbonara is a classic dish, but I have refined it here by using bite-sized pieces of Parma ham and a sauce that is just a light emulsion of eggs and cheese. You could use prosciutto or Serrano instead of the Parma ham.

1] Preheat the grill to high and line the grill rack with foil. Grill the Parma ham for 4–5 minutes until crisp. Leave to cool on a plate lined with kitchen paper, then break the Parma ham into bite-sized pieces and leave to one side.

2] Meanwhile, cook the spaghetti in a large saucepan of boiling salted water for 12 minutes or until al dente.

3] Put the egg yolks and Parmesan in a bowl and whisk to combine.

4] Put the oil, butter and half of the Parma ham pieces in a large, deep frying pan. Heat over a medium-low heat until the butter melts.

5] Now you need to work quickly. Drain the pasta, reserving 250ml/9fl oz/1 cup of the cooking water. Add the cooked pasta to the frying pan and turn off the heat.

6] Whisk 4 tablespoons of the pasta cooking water into the egg yolk mixture, then add to the frying pan. Toss everything together with a further 4 tablespoons of the pasta cooking water to make a thin, smooth sauce. Add a splash of extra water if the sauce is too thick. Season to taste with salt and pepper. You may not need extra salt as the ham is quite salty.

7] Scatter the remaining Parma ham over the pasta and serve sprinkled with parsley and extra Parmesan.

"SHOW ME HOW" TO GRILL THE PARMA HAM

HOME FAVOURITES

4 tbsp vegetable oil
6 sage leaves, thinly sliced
3 garlic cloves, 2 thinly sliced and 1 crushed
50g/1¾oz unsalted butter, softened
4 pork chops or loin chops, each about
  300g/10½oz

salt and freshly ground black pepper
1 recipe quantity Chunky Chips
  (see page 215), Wilted Spinach (see page 218)
  and lemon wedges, to serve

SERVES 4 | **PREPARATION TIME** 35 minutes | **COOKING TIME** 15 minutes

GRILLED GARLIC & SAGE PORK CHOPS

Both garlic and sage are natural partners with pork, and you get a double whammy in this recipe with an infused oil as well as a flavoured butter. I love to dip my chips into the sage butter as it melts over the hot pork chop.

1] Put the oil, 4 of the sage leaves and the sliced garlic into a small saucepan. Put the pan over a low heat and warm the oil until the garlic and sage just start to sizzle. Take the pan off the heat and leave the oil to infuse for 30 minutes.

2] Meanwhile, put the remaining sage and the crushed garlic into a bowl and mix in the butter until combined. Put the flavoured butter on a piece of cling film and roll up to form a small log shape, then twist the ends to seal. Put the wrapped butter log in the freezer for 10–15 minutes to firm up.

3] Preheat the grill to high. Brush the chops with the sage oil and season well with salt and pepper. Grill the chops for 4–6 minutes on each side until the fat is golden but the pork is still slightly pink in the middle.

4] Transfer the chops to warm plates. Slice the butter log into 4 and put one pat on top of each chop. Serve with chunky chips, wilted spinach and lemon wedges.

JOHNNIE'S TIP

Pork chops can be a little dry at times but are improved by a nice long soak in a flavoured brine. Dissolve 4 tablespoons salt and 4 tablespoons soft light brown sugar in 150ml/5fl oz/scant ⅔ cup boiling water. Add 500ml/17fl oz/2 cups apple juice, 250ml/9fl oz/1 cup cold water, 2 sliced garlic cloves and 4 sage sprigs. Leave the brine to cool completely. Put the chops in a deep dish and pour the brine over. Cover and refrigerate for 8 hours, or overnight. Remove the chops from the brine and pat dry with kitchen paper before cooking.

250g/9oz cooking chorizo, cut into
   bite-sized pieces
1 onion, thinly sliced
1 red pepper, deseeded and diced
1 fat garlic clove, crushed
a pinch of saffron
250g/9oz/1¼ cups easy-cook long-grain rice
500ml/17fl oz/2 cups hot vegetable stock

100g/3½oz/⅔ cup frozen peas
225g/8oz large raw, shell-on prawns
8–12 mussels, prepared and rinsed (discard
   any shells that remain open when tapped)
a squeeze of lemon juice
1 handful of parsley leaves, roughly chopped
salt and freshly ground black pepper
lemon wedges, to serve

SERVES 4 | **PREPARATION TIME** 25 minutes | **COOKING TIME** 40 minutes

PAELLA WITH CHORIZO & PRAWNS

Long-grain rice is used in this recipe, rather than the usual short, stocky Spanish rice. This means the rice grains stay separate when cooked, ensuring you get a little taste of everything with each mouthful.

1] Put the chorizo in a large sauté pan over a medium heat. Cook for 4–5 minutes until the chorizo has released its orange oil. Add the onion, pepper and garlic and cook gently for 8–10 minutes, stirring occasionally, until softened.

2] Add the saffron and rice to the pan and stir to coat the rice in the chorizo oil. Season with salt and pepper, then add enough of the stock to just cover the rice. Bring to the boil, then turn the heat down to low and simmer for about 15 minutes until the rice is almost cooked but still has a slight bite. Add extra stock if the pan gets too dry, but do not stir.

3] Scatter the peas over the top and nestle the prawns and mussels into the rice. Cook for a further 8–10 minutes until the prawns have cooked through and the mussels have opened. During this time, don't stir the paella but move the pan around over the heat periodically so that the paella cooks evenly. A crust may form on the bottom of the pan; this is called *socorrat* and is considered a delicacy.

4] Remove any mussels that have not opened during cooking and discard them. Squeeze over a little lemon juice and check the seasoning. Serve the paella direct from the pan with chopped parsley scattered over the top and lemon wedges.

250g/9oz/1¼ cups long-grain rice

2 boneless pork loin steaks, each about 150g/5½oz, fat trimmed

a large pinch of cayenne pepper

4 tbsp soy sauce

4 tbsp soft dark brown sugar

4 tbsp vegetable oil

4 shallots, thinly sliced

2 garlic cloves, thinly sliced

2.5cm/1in piece fresh ginger, peeled and grated

2 fresh green bird's eye chillies, thinly sliced

250g/9oz/heaped 1½ cups frozen peas

4 eggs

1 handful of coriander leaves, roughly chopped

4 spring onions, thinly sliced

chilli or Tabasco sauce (optional), to serve

SERVES 4 | PREPARATION TIME 45 minutes, plus chilling | COOKING TIME 30 minutes

PORK WITH EGG-FRIED RICE

This is a really great variation on the Indonesian classic of *nasi goreng*, which rumour has it was enjoyed by Barack Obama during his state visit to Indonesia in 2010.

1] Put the rice in a saucepan and cover with plenty of cold water. Bring to the boil, then turn the heat down and simmer for 10 minutes or until tender. Drain and spread the rice over a large platter for 20 minutes to cool. Transfer the rice to a lidded container and refrigerate for at least 4 hours or overnight before using.

2] Cover the pork steaks with cling film and beat with a meat mallet or rolling pin until 3mm/⅛in thick. Cut the pork into little finger-sized slices. Transfer to a bowl, dust with the cayenne pepper and leave to one side. Mix together the soy sauce and sugar, then leave to one side.

3] Heat 1 tablespoon of the oil in a large wok or frying pan over a medium heat. Add the shallots and stir-fry for 5–6 minutes until golden. Add the garlic, ginger and chillies and stir-fry for a further 2 minutes. Turn the heat to high, add the pork and stir-fry for 2–3 minutes until the pork has turned opaque, then add the cooked rice and the peas. Stir-fry for 5–6 minutes until the peas have thawed and the rice is piping hot. Stir in the soy sauce mixture, remove from the heat and keep warm.

4] Heat the remaining oil in a large frying pan over a medium heat. When shimmering, crack the eggs into the pan and fry for 2–3 minutes until cooked to your liking.

5] Stir the coriander into the rice and divide into 4 bowls. Sit a fried egg on top and scatter over the spring onions. Serve immediately with some chilli sauce.

JOHNNIE'S TIP

This would be good made using leftover Chinese Barbecue Pork (see page 133) or Korean-style Fiery Pork (see page 130). Add at the same time as the rice, since the pork in both recipes is already cooked.

450g/1lb pork loin steaks, fat trimmed

1 tbsp cornflour

3 tbsp tomato ketchup

225g/8oz tinned pineapple rings in natural juice, drained and cut into 1cm/½in pieces, and 3 tbsp juice reserved

1½ tbsp sweet chilli sauce

1½ tsp rice wine vinegar, plus extra to taste

1½ tsp soft light brown sugar, plus extra to taste

2 tbsp vegetable oil

1 red pepper, deseeded and cut into 1cm/½in squares

1 green pepper, deseeded and cut into 1cm/½in squares

1 bunch of spring onions, trimmed and cut into into 2cm/¾in pieces

1 garlic clove, crushed

½cm/¼in piece fresh ginger, peeled and finely chopped

steamed jasmine rice, to serve

SERVES 4 | **PREPARATION TIME** 20 minutes | **COOKING TIME** 10 minutes

SWEET & SOUR PORK

Sweet and sour pork is probably one of the most popular dishes in Chinese restaurants and takeaways, but it can be disappointing with heavily battered pork and a glutinous, bland sauce. My version is neither of these, having a light, crisp batter and a slightly spicy, light sauce.

1] Cover the pork steaks with cling film and beat with a meat mallet or rolling pin until about 2mm/¹⁄₁₆in thick. Cut the pork into 1cm/½in squares and transfer to a bowl. Dust with the cornflour and leave to one side.

2] Whisk the ketchup, tinned pineapple juice, sweet chilli sauce, vinegar and sugar together in a jug and set aside.

3] Heat 1 tablespoon of the oil in a large wok or frying pan over a high heat. When the oil is shimmering, add the red and green peppers and the spring onions and stir-fry for about 4 minutes until the vegetables have softened. Transfer to a bowl and set aside.

4] Heat the remaining oil in the wok for a few seconds, then add the garlic and ginger and let them sizzle for 30 seconds. Add the pork and stir-fry for 2 minutes or until the pork is almost cooked. Return the vegetables to the pan with the pineapple. Pour in the ketchup mixture and cook, stirring, for 1–2 minutes until the sauce is just hot. Remove from the heat and taste, adding more vinegar or sugar, if needed. Serve the pork with bowls of jasmine rice.

400ml/14fl oz/generous 1½ cups tinned
    coconut milk
125ml/4fl oz/½ cup vegetable stock
115g/4oz green beans, halved
700g/1lb 9oz pork loin steaks, fat trimmed,
    cut into bite-sized pieces
1–2 tsp fish sauce
1–2 tsp sugar
a squeeze of lime juice
1 handful of coriander leaves
thick rice noodles or steamed jasmine
    rice, to serve

2 black peppercorns
1 tsp cumin seeds
1 tsp coriander seeds
3 fresh green bird's eye chillies, roughly
    chopped
1 shallot, roughly chopped
2 garlic cloves, roughly chopped
stalks from 1 bunch of coriander
1 handful of coriander leaves
2.5cm/1in piece galangal or 1cm/½in piece
    fresh ginger, peeled and chopped
2 kaffir lime leaves
½ lemongrass stalk, tough outer leaves
    removed, roughly chopped
1 tsp fish sauce
juice of ½ lime

SERVES 4 | **PREPARATION TIME** 30 minutes | **COOKING TIME** 20 minutes

THAI GREEN CURRY WITH PORK

**You can make double the quantity of curry paste and freeze half of it for future use,
or use in the Pork & Lemongrass Wraps (see page 120).**

1] To make the Thai green curry paste, toast the peppercorns, cumin and coriander seeds
in a dry frying pan for 3–4 minutes until fragrant. Cool slightly and grind to a powder
using a mini food processor or pestle and mortar. Add the remaining curry paste
ingredients and process to a coarse paste.

2] To make the curry, bring 4 tablespoons of the coconut milk to the boil in a large wok
or sauté pan. Boil for a few minutes until it separates, then add the curry paste and
cook for 2 more minutes. Stir in the rest of the coconut milk and the stock.

3] Bring to the boil, add the green beans and boil for 2 minutes. Add the pork, turn the
heat down to low and gently simmer the pork for 5–6 minutes until just cooked. Don't
let the curry boil, as the pork will become tough. Remove the wok from the heat.

4] Add 1 teaspoon each of the fish sauce and sugar as well as a squeeze of lime, then return
the pan to the heat for 1 minute. Taste and add more fish sauce, sugar and lime juice as
needed. Sprinkle the curry with coriander and serve with rice noodles.

450g/1lb pork loin steaks, fat trimmed

1 tsp paprika

30g/1oz unsalted butter

4 shallots, thinly sliced

450g/1lb chestnut mushrooms, thinly sliced

1 fat garlic clove, crushed

150ml/5fl oz/scant ⅔ cup beef stock

1 tbsp vegetable oil

2 tbsp brandy

300ml/10½fl oz/scant 1¼ cups crème fraîche

1 tsp Worcestershire sauce

2 tsp Dijon mustard

1 small handful of flat-leaf parsley leaves, chopped

salt and freshly ground black pepper

basmati or jasmine rice, to serve

SERVES 4 | **PREPARATION TIME** 10 minutes, plus marinating | **COOKING TIME** 25 minutes

PORK STROGANOFF

A kick-back to the 80s, but with pork! It tastes just as good as the beef version and, of course, it's better value.

1] Cover the pork steaks with cling film and beat with a meat mallet or rolling pin until about 5mm/¼in thick. Cut the pork into little finger-sized strips and transfer to a bowl. Toss the pork in the paprika and leave to marinate for about 30–35 minutes.

2] Melt the butter in a large, deep frying pan over a medium heat. When the butter is foaming, add the shallots and cook for 3–4 minutes until softened. Add the mushrooms and cook for about 5 minutes until tender and any liquid coming from them has evaporated. Add the garlic and cook for a further 1 minute.

3] Pour in the stock, increase the heat to high, then boil until it has almost evaporated and looks syrupy. Transfer the mushroom mixture to a bowl.

4] Put the oil in the frying pan and return it to a high heat. When the oil is shimmering, add the pork and spread it out evenly in the pan. Season with salt and cook for about 3 minutes until browned on the underside but still slightly pink on top, then stir in the brandy and either carefully flame the brandy or let it boil until evaporated. Add the mushroom mixture and reduce the heat to very low.

5] Stir in the crème fraîche, Worcestershire sauce and mustard, then season with salt and pepper. Heat very gently until the sauce is warmed through, then scatter the parsley over and serve with rice.

"SHOW ME HOW" TO TRIM AND BROWN THE PORK

2 tbsp vegetable oil

750g/1lb 10oz boneless pork leg, cut into 2.5cm/1in cubes

1 onion, thinly sliced

1 garlic clove, crushed

½ tsp ground coriander

½ tsp ground cumin

1cm/½in piece fresh ginger, peeled and grated

½ tsp ground allspice

1 fresh red chilli, deseeded and diced

a pinch of crushed dried chillies

800g/1lb 12oz tinned chopped tomatoes

1 tbsp clear honey

200g/7oz ready-to-eat dried apricots

1 handful of coriander leaves, finely chopped

salt and freshly ground black pepper

PISTACHIO COUSCOUS

250g/9oz/1⅓ cups couscous

3 tbsp olive oil

2 tbsp lemon juice

55g/2oz/⅓ cup shelled unsalted pistachios, roughly chopped

6 spring onions, thinly sliced

SERVES 4 | PREPARATION TIME 20 minutes | COOKING TIME 1 hour 50 minutes

PORK & APRICOT TAGINE

What a cracker – pork with fruit is a winner every time!

1] Put 1 tablespoon of the oil in a large cast iron casserole or heavy-based saucepan over a medium heat. When the oil is shimmering, add the pork and cook for 5–6 minutes, turning it regularly, until browned on the outside. Transfer to a plate and set to one side.

2] Add the remaining oil to the pan and cook the onion for 8–10 minutes, stirring occasionally, until softened and slightly browned at the edges. Return the pork to the pan and stir in the garlic, ground coriander, cumin, ginger, allspice and both types of chilli. Cook for 2 minutes, then add the tomatoes and honey. Bring to the boil, then turn the heat down to low, cover the pan and simmer for 45 minutes.

3] Remove the lid, add the apricots and increase the heat slightly. Cook for a further 45 minutes, uncovered, until the apricots are soft and the pork is tender; season to taste.

4] Meanwhile, put the couscous in a bowl and cover with 400ml/14fl oz/generous 1½ cups just-boiled water. Cover and leave to stand for 10 minutes until the water is absorbed. Fluff up the grains with a fork, then stir in the olive oil, lemon juice, pistachios and spring onions, then season. Scatter the coriander over the tagine and serve with the couscous.

12 ready-to-eat dried prunes

6 tbsp good brandy

500g/1lb 2oz pork tenderloin fillet, fat and silverskin membrane trimmed, cut into 1cm/½in thick slices

40g/1½oz unsalted butter

1 tsp vegetable oil

200ml/7fl oz/scant 1 cup crème fraîche

2 tsp Dijon mustard

a squeeze of lemon juice

2 tbsp chopped walnuts

salt and freshly ground black pepper

1 recipe quantity Green Beans with Garlic & Almonds (see page 218) and steamed new potatoes, to serve

SERVES 4 | PREPARATION TIME 10 minutes, plus cooling | COOKING TIME 15 minutes

PORK MEDALLIONS WITH BRANDY-SOAKED PRUNES

A match made in heaven! The heavily scented aroma of the brandy infused into the prunes adds an extra dimension to this amazing dish.

1] Put the prunes in a small saucepan with 2 tablespoons of the brandy and 2 tablespoons water. Bring to the boil over a medium heat, then turn the heat down and simmer for 5 minutes until the prunes are soft and plump. Leave them to cool for 20 minutes.

2] Meanwhile, cover the pork with cling film and beat with a meat mallet or rolling pin until about 5mm/¼in thick. Season with salt and pepper.

3] Heat the butter and oil in a large frying pan over a medium-high heat. When the butter is foaming, add the pork medallions and cook for 2 minutes until browned and slightly crusted on the base, then turn over and cook for another 1 minute.

4] Add the remaining brandy and let it boil for 2 minutes until reduced by half and the alcohol evaporates. Remove the pan from the heat and stir in the crème fraîche, mustard and prunes. Return the pan to a very low heat and gently warm the cream through, making sure it doesn't boil. Season with salt, pepper and a squeeze of lemon juice.

5] Spoon the prunes and the sauce over the pork medallions. Scatter the walnuts over and serve with new potatoes and green beans with garlic and almonds.

2 pork tenderloin fillets, each about 450g/1lb,
    fat and silverskin membrane trimmed
30g/1oz unsalted butter
2 tsp vegetable oil
1 shallot, very finely chopped
250ml/9fl oz/1 cup dry white wine
150ml/5fl oz/scant ⅔ cup vegetable stock

1 tbsp wholegrain mustard, or to taste
6 tbsp crème fraîche
salt and freshly ground black pepper
1 recipe quantity Johnnie's Mashed Potatoes
    (see page 215) and Wilted Spinach (see page
    218), to serve

SERVES 4–6 | **PREPARATION TIME** 10 minutes | **COOKING TIME** 35 minutes

PORK TENDERLOIN WITH MUSTARD SAUCE

Pork's mild flavour is a good canvas for this punchy grainy mustard sauce. Cook it until it is slightly pink in the centre.

1] If you like, you can trim the ends of each fillet so that they are a uniform thickness with neat ends. Season the fillets with a generous amount of salt and pepper.

2] Heat the butter and oil in a large frying pan over a medium-high heat. When the butter is foaming, add the pork fillets and cook until browned all over, including the ends. Add the shallot and cook for 2 minutes until softened slightly.

3] Pour the wine and stock into the pan. Bring to the boil, then turn the heat down and simmer for 1 minute. Cover the pan and cook for 20 minutes, turning the pork every 5 minutes. If the liquid is boiling madly, then reduce the heat a little more – the pork will become stringy if you let it boil too hard. It should be cooked to just pink in the centre after 20 minutes. You can check this by sticking a small, sharp knife or skewer into the centre of one of the fillets. If the juices are red then cook the pork for a further 5 minutes and check again until they run clear.

4] Transfer the pork to a plate and cover with foil. Boil the liquid in the pan until reduced by half, then turn the heat down to low. Stir in the mustard and crème fraîche and warm though for a couple of minutes without boiling.

5] Slice the pork into medallions and serve with the sauce, mashed potatoes and spinach.

JOHNNIE'S TIP

To get perfectly round circles of pork, tie the tenderloins at 3cm/1¼in intervals with cook's string. Wrap the tenderloins in cling film, twist the ends like a Christmas cracker to secure, then put in the fridge overnight. Unwrap and cook the pork as detailed in the recipe above.

"SHOW ME HOW" TO PREPARE AND COOK THE TENDERLOIN

1.25kg/2lb 12oz boneless loin of pork

100g/3½oz/½ cup good-quality black olives, pitted

30g/1oz basil leaves

30g/1oz/scant ¼ cup lightly toasted pine nuts

125g/4½oz/½ cup ricotta

finely grated zest of 1 lemon

1 tsp vegetable oil

1 tsp sea salt flakes

fine salt and freshly ground pepper

1 recipe quantity Creamy Gravy (see page 212), Goose Fat Roast Potatoes (see page 216) and steamed green beans, to serve

SERVES 4 | PREPARATION TIME 30 minutes, plus resting | COOKING TIME 1½ hours

ROLLED LOIN OF PORK WITH RICOTTA & BASIL

1] Score the skin of the pork loin at 1cm/½in intervals then turn it over. The loin should have a small flap of belly that flops to one side. Turn the pork until this flap is on the right, then use a sharp knife to make a horizontal cut through the flesh of the pork loin. Cut about three-quarters of the way through the loin, then open it out like a book. Cover in cling film and beat with a meat mallet or rolling pin until you have a rectangular piece of pork, about 1cm/½in thick. Remove the cling film and set aside.

2] Put the olives in a food processor with the basil leaves and pine nuts and pulse until finely chopped. Add the ricotta and lemon zest, then season and pulse again to mix.

3] Season the pork with salt and pepper, then spread the ricotta mixture on top. Roll the loin up from left to right and turn it over so the seam is underneath. Secure by tying 4–5 pieces of string around the joint. Rub the vegetable oil over the skin and sprinkle with the sea salt flakes. Put the pork on a wire rack set over a roasting tin and leave to one side while you preheat the oven to 220°C/425°F/Gas 7.

4] Roast the pork for 25 minutes, then reduce the temperature to 180°C/350°F/Gas 4 and cook for a further 1 hour, turning the pan around halfway through the cooking time. (If your joint of pork is a different size, cook at 180°C/350°F/Gas 4 for 22 minutes per 450g/1lb.) Remove the pork from the oven, transfer it to a plate and leave to rest in a warm place for 20 minutes. Snip away the string and serve the pork with the creamy gravy, goose fat roast potatoes and green beans.

JOHNNIE'S TIP

For extra-crispy crackling, turn the oven back up to 220°C/425°F/Gas 7 when you take the pork out. Snip the string and cut off the crackling. Put on a baking sheet and roast for 15–20 minutes.

"SHOW ME HOW" TO STUFF, ROLL AND TIE THE PORK LOIN

CHAPTER 2

CURED, DRIED, PRESERVED & SMOKED

There are various ways to preserve pork, many of which have been used for centuries. Curing is one method, and its big advantage when used in cooking is that it adds lots of flavour. Air-cured, or dried, hams also add a savoury depth of flavour, or "umami", which brings an extra dimension to dishes such as the Serrano Ham with Roasted Figs & Hazelnuts – the perfect blend of sweet fruit, savoury meat and creamy ricotta.

When smoked, bacon and pancetta are irresistible eaten on their own. However, adding them to blander ingredients can completely lift a dish, such as the Pancetta & Pea Risotto or Pasta Amatriciana. The fat in these cuts can also be rendered in a hot pan and used for frying, or will keep meat moist if used as a wrapping, such as in the Pancetta-wrapped Pork with Mushroom Stuffing.

When most people think of ham they think of a large joint but smaller smoked ham hocks are cheap and versatile. In this chapter, the hock is used in dishes such as Parma Ham & Pea Terrines or Ham Hock with Pinto Beans. It also infuses the cooking liquid with a delicious flavour and can be used as a stock for the Ham Hock Broth with Kale, making a single cut of meat go a very long way.

This chapter also explains in a simple, no-fuss way how to smoke or cure your own meat with recipes for Hot-smoked Pork Tenderloin as well as a flavoursome Home-cured Bacon with Maple & Juniper.

250g/9oz cooking chorizo, cut into small chunks

1 red onion, very finely chopped

½ red pepper, deseeded and finely diced

800g/1lb 12oz tinned chopped tomatoes

¼ tsp dried oregano

¼ tsp sugar

1 tbsp vegetable oil

4 eggs

4 slices of country-style bread, such as sourdough

chopped coriander leaves, to serve

salt and freshly ground pepper

SERVES 4 | **PREPARATION TIME** 15 minutes | **COOKING TIME** 50 minutes

CHORIZO RANCHEROS

Huevos rancheros is a popular breakfast dish in Mexico. I like to add spicy, smoky chorizo to the tomato sauce to give it extra substance, then serve it topped with a fried egg. You can also take the more traditional route of baking the eggs in the sauce if you want to make individual portions.

1] Put the chorizo in a large, deep frying pan over a medium heat. Cook for 4–5 minutes until the oil has been released from the chorizo and it is sizzling slightly. Add the onion and pepper and cook for 10 minutes, stirring frequently, until softened. Add the tomatoes, oregano and sugar. Bring to the boil, then turn the heat down and simmer for 25–30 minutes until reduced and thickened. Season to taste with salt and pepper.

2] Meanwhile, heat the vegetable oil in a separate large frying pan and fry the eggs until the whites are set and the yolks remain runny. Toast the bread on both sides.

3] Spoon the sauce over the slices of toast, sit the fried eggs on top and serve sprinkled with the coriander.

20 slices of pancetta, about 110g/3¾oz
   total weight
30g/1oz unsalted butter
4 shallots, finely chopped
3 garlic cloves, crushed
¾ tsp dried thyme
350g/12oz pig's liver, coarsely minced
350g/12oz lean pork loin, coarsely minced
350g/12oz pork fat, coarsely minced

3 tbsp brandy
3 tbsp double cream
1 egg, lightly beaten
½ tsp ground allspice
1 tbsp drained green peppercorns in brine
vegetable oil, for frying
salt and freshly ground black pepper
toast, cornichons and pickle, to serve

SERVES 14–16 | **PREPARATION TIME** 30 minutes, plus cooling and 24 hours pressing | **COOKING TIME** 2¼ hours

ARDENNES PÂTÉ

This coarse pâté is not usually wrapped in pancetta, but I like the extra flavour it adds. The pork, liver and fat need to be coarsely minced, which is easy to do in a food processor.

1] Preheat the oven to 150°C/300°F/Gas 2. Line the base and sides of a 900g/2lb loaf tin or terrine dish with pancetta, arranging the slices widthways and leaving some overhang.

2] Melt the butter in a small frying pan over a medium heat. Add the shallots and cook for 4–5 minutes until softened, then add the garlic and thyme and cook for a further 1 minute. Transfer to a bowl and add all of the remaining ingredients. Season with salt and pepper. Check the seasoning by frying a teaspoonful in a small frying pan, remembering that the pâté will taste less seasoned once it is cold, so you may need to add a little more than you first think.

3] Pack the pâté mixture into the prepared loaf tin and fold the overhanging pieces of pancetta over the top. Cover the tin with foil and put it in a small, deep roasting tin. Fill the roasting tin with enough water from a just-boiled kettle to come three-quarters of the way up the sides of the loaf tin.

4] Put the pâté in its water bath in the oven and cook for 1½ hours. Uncover the pâté, top up the water if it is very low and cook for a further 30 minutes. Check the pâté is cooked by inserting a thin, sharp knife or skewer into the centre; it is ready when the juices run clear. If you have a meat thermometer, the internal temperature of the pâté should be 72°C/161°F. If it's not ready, cook for a further 15 minutes and check again.

5] Remove the loaf tin from the water bath and leave to cool in the tin. When cool, cover the loaf tin with cling film or foil, press by sitting a couple of cans on top, and put it in the fridge for 24 hours before turning out. Serve the pâté with toast, cornichons and your favourite pickle.

300g/10½oz goose or duck fat
500g/1lb 2oz pork shoulder steaks, cut into
   2.5cm/1in cubes
3 tbsp Calvados or brandy
10 black peppercorns
6 juniper berries
4 cloves

3 thyme sprigs
6 parsley sprigs
2 bay leaves
salt and freshly ground black pepper
thin slices of toast, small pickled onions
   and cornichons, to serve

SERVES 8 | PREPARATION TIME 30 minutes, plus cooling and 24 hours chilling |
COOKING TIME 4 hours

GOOSE FAT POTTED PORK

Shred the cubes of slow-cooked meat to create a great coarse-textured potted meat.

1] Melt the goose or duck fat in a medium-sized cast iron casserole or heavy-based saucepan over a low heat.

2] When melted, add the pork, Calvados, peppercorns, juniper berries, cloves and the herbs, plus enough water to just cover the meat. Bring to the boil, then turn the heat down to as low as possible, cover the pan and cook for 4 hours until the meat is falling apart into shreds. Check the pan regularly to make sure it is not boiling: the surface should just be trembling and you may need to top it up with extra water.

3] Remove the pan from the heat and leave the pork to cool to room temperature, about 2 hours. Carefully lift the pieces of pork from the pan and, using 2 forks back to back, shred into a bowl. Season generously with salt and pepper, as the potted pork will taste less seasoned when cold. Pack the meat into 2 x 300ml/10½fl oz/scant 1¼ cups sterilized preserving jars or 8 x 150ml/5fl oz/⅔ cup ramekins. Strain the cooking liquid, discarding the peppercorns, juniper berries, cloves and the herbs, then spoon it over the meat to cover by about ½cm/¼in.

4] Cover the potted pork with cling film or a lid and refrigerate until needed. They will improve with keeping, so try to leave them for at least 24 hours before serving. (The potted pork will keep for up to 1 month in the fridge, as long as the meat is fully covered by the fat and not exposed to the air.)

5] Remove from the fridge about 30 minutes before serving with thin slices of toast, small pickled onions and cornichons.

"SHOW ME HOW" TO SHRED AND POT THE PORK

1 smoked ham hock, about 750g/1lb 10oz
   total weight
1 carrot, halved
1 onion, halved
1 celery stalk, halved
4 black peppercorns
1 bay leaf
3–4 parsley sprigs

75g/2½oz/½ cup frozen peas
8 cornichons, finely chopped
1 handful of flat-leaf parsley leaves, finely
   chopped
8 slices of Parma ham or prosciutto crudo
freshly ground black pepper
thin slices of toast, to serve

SERVES 4 | **PREPARATION TIME** 20 minutes, plus cooling and overnight chilling | **COOKING TIME** 4½ hours

PARMA HAM & PEA TERRINES

Peas and ham have a natural affinity, and these little terrines make an attractive light summer lunch.

1] Put the ham hock, carrot, onion and celery in a large saucepan and pour in enough cold water to cover by 2cm/¾in (about 2l/70fl oz/8 cups). Bring to the boil over a medium heat, skimming off any foamy scum that rises to the surface. Turn the heat down to low.

2] Add the peppercorns, bay leaf and parsley stalks, part-cover with a lid, then simmer very gently for 4 hours or until the ham starts to fall away from the bone. Transfer the ham to a plate and leave to cool.

3] Strain the cooking liquid through a fine sieve into a clean saucepan, discarding the vegetables, peppercorns, bay leaf and parsley sprigs. Bring to the boil, then cook until reduced to 300ml/10½fl oz/scant 1¼ cups. Leave to one side to cool.

4] Boil the peas for 1 minute, then drain and refresh under cold running water. Drain again and leave to one side.

5] Pull the ham away from the bone, discarding any fat and skin. Tear the ham into small pieces and put it in a large bowl with the peas, cornichons and chopped parsley. Season with pepper, but don't use salt as the reduced cooking liquid has enough seasoning.

6] Line 4 x 200ml/7fl oz/scant 1 cup ramekins with the Parma ham, leaving some overhang. Divide the ham mixture between the ramekins, pressing it down firmly. Add just enough of the reduced liquid to cover the ham mixture, then fold the Parma ham over the top to cover the surface. Put them in the fridge for 1 hour to chill. Cover each ramekin with cling film, put a small weight on top (you could use ramekins or small coffee cups filled with baking beans) and refrigerate overnight.

7] To serve, run a knife around the rim of each terrine and turn out onto a plate. Serve with slices of toast.

CURED, DRIED, PRESERVED & SMOKED

5 eggs

8 slices of white bread (thin or medium)

8 slices of Parma ham

8 sun-blush tomatoes, drained if in oil and sliced

250g/8oz mozzarella cheese, drained and cut into 1cm/$\frac{1}{4}$in slices

8 basil leaves

40g/1$\frac{1}{2}$oz unsalted butter, plus extra, if needed

salt and freshly ground black pepper

2 handfuls of rocket leaves, to serve

SERVES 4 | **PREPARATION TIME** 10 minutes | **COOKING TIME** 15 minutes

PARMA HAM, MOZZARELLA & SUN-DRIED TOMATOES IN CARROZZA

This *carrozza* is the ultimate toasted sarni and there's no need for an electric sandwich maker! The filling is a great mix of sweet tomatoes, salty Parma ham and unctuous mozzarella – perfect.

1] Break the eggs into a shallow dish, season with salt and pepper and whisk until frothy.

2] Set out 4 slices of bread and lay 2 slices of ham on each, folding the ham to fit and leaving a small border of bread around the edge. Top with the sun-blush tomatoes and mozzarella in a single layer (you may not need all of the cheese, depending on the size of the bread). Sit the basil leaves on the mozzarella. Brush a little of the beaten egg over the edge of the bread, then top with a second slice of bread, pressing down firmly. (If you are being fancy, you can remove the crusts, or even cut each sandwich into a large circle using a round cutter.)

3] Melt the butter in a large frying pan over a medium heat. Dip each sandwich in the beaten egg, turning until coated. When the butter is foaming, gently slide 2 sandwiches into the pan, ham-side down. Fry for 2–3 minutes until golden on the underside. Using a spatula, carefully turn the sandwiches over and fry for a further 3 minutes until golden brown on both sides. Repeat with the remaining sandwiches, adding more butter if necessary. Turn the heat down if the bread is browning too quickly, because the cheese needs to be given time to heat through and melt. Serve the sandwiches with rocket leaves.

HOW TO SMOKE PORK

Home-smoking isn't as challenging as it sounds, and it is even possible to make your own smoker from regular kitchen equipment. It's basically no more than a lidded container – you can use a covered charcoal barbecue, a wok or even buy a simple smoker, but if you want to try smoking without investing in a lot of kit, it's feasible to make a basic smoker from a small roasting tin, a rack and some aluminium foil.

Special smoking wood chips are required and you need to make sure they are free of pesticides, as well as cut into small chips that will smoke for a good amount of time. The type of wood can be varied to give different flavours and many are now available to buy online.

Smoking times will depend on the cut of the meat – a large piece can take several hours, while a small fillet can be done quickly – but both taste great with a fragrant smokiness.

---

2 pork tenderloin fillets, about 450g/1lb each, fat and silverskin membrane trimmed
2 tsp smoked paprika
2 tsp soft light brown sugar
½ tsp dried oregano

½ tsp salt
¼ tsp ground black pepper

YOU WILL ALSO NEED
smoking chips, preferably hickory

SERVES 4 | PREPARATION TIME 30 minutes, plus marinating and overnight cooling | COOKING TIME 20 minutes

HOT-SMOKED PORK TENDERLOIN

1] Put the pork fillets on a large piece of cling film. Mix together the smoked paprika, sugar, oregano, salt and pepper and rub the mixture over the pork fillets. Wrap the fillets tightly in the cling film and leave to marinate in the fridge for 8 hours, or overnight.

2] To make a stove-top smoker, you need a medium-sized, heavy-based roasting tin with a wire rack that fits inside; a grill pan is ideal. Cover the base with a layer of smoking chips (you can line the tin with foil to protect it) and sit the wire rack on top. Put the pork fillets on the rack and cover with a double layer of foil, making sure it is sealed very tightly around the edges to keep in the smoke.

3] Put the smoker over a high heat for 3–4 minutes. When you see the odd wisp of smoke, turn the heat to low and cook for 12 minutes. Turn off the heat and leave to stand for 2 minutes before opening the foil. The pork should be cooked through, but if it is very pink and bloody in the centre, you will need to pan-fry the fillets for 8–10 minutes. Leave the fillets to cool, then cover and refrigerate overnight before serving thinly sliced as part of a charcuterie platter. They will keep for up to 4 days stored in the fridge.

50g/1¾oz/heaped ⅓ cup hazelnuts

4 large or 8 small figs

2 tsp clear honey

125g/4½oz mascarpone

1–2 tbsp milk

8 slices Serrano ham, about 100g/3½oz
  total weight

1 handful of rocket leaves

2 tbsp hazelnut or extra virgin
  olive oil

juice of ½ lemon

salt and freshly ground pepper

country-style bread, lightly charred
  on a griddle pan, to serve (optional)

SERVES 4 (as a starter) | **PREPARATION TIME** 15 minutes | **COOKING TIME** 35 minutes

SERRANO HAM WITH ROASTED FIGS & HAZELNUTS

A perfect combination of taste and texture – sweet figs, salty ham, with a crunch from the hazelnuts.

1] Preheat the oven to 150°C/300°F/Gas 2. Put the hazelnuts on a baking sheet and roast for 20–25 minutes until lightly browned. You should just start to smell a hazelnut aroma. Remove the nuts from the oven and increase the temperature to 220°C/425°F/Gas 7.

2] If the hazelnuts have their skins on, transfer them to a clean tea towel and rub vigorously until the skins come off. Using a rolling pin, roughly crush the nuts, then leave to one side.

3] Cut a cross in the top of each fig, cutting about halfway down towards the base. Stand the figs upright on a baking sheet and drizzle the honey over. Roast for 5–10 minutes until the figs have warmed through and softened a little. The timing will depend on the ripeness of your figs – riper ones will soften very quickly.

4] Mix half of the hazelnuts with the mascarpone, adding the milk to soften the mixture slightly. Put it in a pot or bowl ready to serve.

5] Serve the ham with the figs, then scatter over the remaining hazelnuts and the rocket leaves. Drizzle the oil and lemon juice over the top, then season with salt and pepper. Serve with the mascarpone cream and slices of griddled bread, if you like.

1 recipe quantity Gnocchi (see page 214), made
  with 1½ tsp freshly ground black pepper
60g/2¼oz unsalted butter
250g/9oz black pudding, skin removed, sliced
  and quartered

16 sage leaves
1 tsp white wine vinegar
4 very fresh large eggs
salt and freshly ground black pepper

SERVES 4 | **PREPARATION TIME** 2 hours (including making the gnocchi) |
COOKING TIME 15 minutes

GNOCCHI WITH BLACK PUDDING & POACHED EGGS

**Pan-frying gnocchi to create an outer "crust" and soft centre adds another dimension
to this already fabulous dish. You might find it easier to part-cook the poached eggs by
cooking them just until the outside of the whites have set, then transferring them to
a bowl of ice-cold water. You can then reheat them in boiling water for 1 minute just
before serving.**

1] Make the gnocchi following the recipe instructions on page 214, adding 1½ teaspoons
of ground black pepper to the dough at the same time as the egg and salt (in step 3).
Put the prepared gnocchi on baking sheets lined with baking paper and dusted with
flour, then leave to one side.

2] Bring a large saucepan of salted water to the boil.

3] Meanwhile, melt the butter in a large frying pan over a medium heat. When the butter
is foaming, add the black pudding and fry for 3–4 minutes until the edges start to crisp.
Remove the frying pan from the heat.

4] Put the gnocchi into the pan of boiling salted water. Return to the boil, then reduce the
heat and simmer for about 4 minutes until cooked. Just before the gnocchi are cooked,
return the frying pan to a medium heat. Using a slotted spoon, remove the gnocchi
from the pan and blot any excess water with kitchen paper before adding them to the
frying pan. Add the sage leaves and cook for 1–2 minutes, adding a splash of the gnocchi
cooking water to give a bit of extra moisture. Cover the pan and keep warm.

5] Bring a large pan of water to the boil and add the vinegar. Crack the eggs, one at a time,
into the pan and poach them for about 2 minutes until the whites are set and the yolks
are still runny. Serve the gnocchi and black pudding topped with a poached egg. Season
with extra black pepper before serving.

1 recipe quantity Gnocchi (see page 214)
8 slices of Serrano ham
4 basil sprigs

PESTO
3 tbsp pine nuts
4 large handfuls of basil leaves

125ml/4fl oz/½ cup olive oil
30g/1oz Grana Padano cheese, finely grated,
    plus extra to serve
1 tbsp lemon juice
salt and freshly ground black pepper

SERVES 4 | **PREPARATION TIME** 2 hours (including making the gnocchi) |
COOKING TIME 15 minutes

GNOCCHI WITH SERRANO HAM & PESTO

Pesto, pesto, pesto! So simple to make, so awful to buy – you really will not believe the difference.

1] Make the gnocchi following the recipe instructions on page 214. Put the prepared gnocchi on baking sheets lined with baking paper and dusted with flour, then leave to one side.

2] To make the pesto, toast the pine nuts in a dry frying pan over a low heat. Set aside to cool completely. Put the basil leaves and oil in a jug and whizz with a hand blender for 2–3 minutes to make a smooth, bright green oil. Crush the cooled pine nuts with the back of a large knife or the heel of your hand and fold into the basil oil with the Grana Padano. Add the lemon juice to slightly cut the oiliness of the sauce, then season to taste with salt and pepper. (You could make the basil oil in a blender or food processor, but stir the pine nuts, Grana Padano and lemon juice in by hand because the heat from the blades can affect their flavour.)

3] Bring a large saucepan of salted water to the boil. Meanwhile, put the Serrano ham into a large, dry frying pan set over a low heat. Cook the ham for 3–4 minutes, turning once, until crisp. Break up 4 of the ham slices and leave them in the frying pan; leave the remaining 4 slices to one side.

4] Put the gnocchi into the pan of salted water and return to the boil, then reduce the heat and simmer for about 4 minutes until cooked. Using a slotted spoon, remove the gnocchi from the pan and blot any excess water with kitchen paper before adding them to the frying pan. Add the pesto and toss the gnocchi, ham and pesto together.

5] Serve the gnocchi and sauce topped with the reserved wafers of crisp Serrano and basil sprigs, with extra Grana Padano sprinkled over.

12 king scallops, about 1–1.5cm/½–¾ in thick

3 tbsp extra virgin olive oil

1 tbsp lemon juice

2 tbsp vegetable oil

300g/10½oz boudin noir or black pudding, casing removed and cut into 12 x 1cm/½in slices

2 large handfuls of rocket leaves

salt and freshly ground black pepper

baguette, to serve

SERVES 4 | **PREPARATION TIME** 15 minutes | **COOKING TIME** 10 minutes

SEARED SCALLOPS WITH BOUDIN NOIR

Scallops and French boudin noir, or black pudding, is a really classic combination. It is worth searching out good-quality black pudding as it has a much smoother texture and superior flavour to the pre-packed sliced alternative.

1] Remove the roe and any hard connective tissue from the scallops. Pat the scallops dry but do not season them at this stage as the salt will draw out moisture.

2] Whisk the olive oil, lemon juice, salt and pepper together in a non-metallic bowl and leave to one side.

3] Put a plate in a warm place and line a second plate with kitchen paper. Heat the vegetable oil in a large, heavy-based frying pan over a high heat. Hold your hand about 15cm/6in above the pan; the pan is ready to use if you can feel the heat. Add the scallops and cook for 1–2 minutes until caramelized on the bottom, then turn over and cook for a further 1–1½ minutes. By this time they should be just cooked in the centre. Don't overcook the scallops as they will become dry and lose their sweetness.

4] Transfer the scallops to the warm plate and cover with foil. Add the boudin noir to the frying pan. Cook for 1½–2 minutes on each side until slightly crusted, then transfer to the lined plate and pat with kitchen paper. Season the scallops with salt and pepper.

5] Whisk the olive oil dressing again and toss with the rocket leaves. Serve the rocket topped with the scallops and boudin noir, with slices of baguette.

250g/9oz/1¼ cups dried pinto beans

1 smoked ham hock, about 1kg/2lb 4oz total weight

1 celery stalk, halved

1 large carrot, scrubbed and halved

1 large onion, quartered

6 black peppercorns

2 bay leaves

6 parsley sprigs

1 tbsp olive oil

1 onion, finely chopped

1 fat garlic clove, crushed

800g/1lb 12oz tinned chopped tomatoes

1 tbsp Dijon mustard

85g/3oz/scant ½ cup dark muscovado sugar

½ tsp dried oregano

salt and freshly ground black pepper

a few coriander leaves and cornbread, to serve

SERVES 4–6 | **PREPARATION TIME** 30 minutes, plus overnight soaking | **COOKING TIME** 5½ hours

HAM HOCK & PINTO BEANS

Yeeeehaaaaa – cowboy beans with style!

1] Put the beans in a large bowl and cover with water. Leave to soak overnight.

2] Put the ham hock in a large saucepan or stockpot and cover with cold water. Add the celery, carrot, quartered onion, peppercorns, bay leaves and parsley sprigs. Bring to the boil over a medium heat, then turn the heat down and simmer, partially covered, for 4 hours until the meat starts to fall away from the bone.

3] About 30 minutes before the ham is cooked, drain the beans. Put the beans in a saucepan and cover with fresh cold water, then bring to the boil over a high heat and boil rapidly for 10 minutes. Drain the beans.

4] Remove the ham hock from the pan and reserve 250ml/9fl oz/1 cup of the cooking liquid. Remove the meat in large chunks from the ham hock and discard any skin or fat.

5] Heat the oil in a large saucepan over a medium heat and cook the chopped onion and garlic for 8–10 minutes until softened. Add the drained beans, tomatoes, mustard, sugar and oregano, plus 125ml/4fl oz/½ cup of the reserved ham cooking liquid. Bring to the boil, then turn the heat down to a simmer.

6] Add the chunks of ham and simmer for 1–1¼ hours until the beans are tender. Stir occasionally, taking care not to break the ham up too much and adding extra cooking liquid, if necessary. Season with pepper and salt, if needed. Serve scattered with a few coriander leaves and with wedges of cornbread.

800g/1lb 12oz white potatoes, peeled and
  coarsely grated
1 onion, coarsely grated
½ tsp salt
1 tbsp plain flour
vegetable oil, for frying
300g/10½oz cherry tomatoes

4 tbsp olive oil
¼ tsp sugar
4 thick slices of Black Forest ham, honey-
  roasted ham or other baked ham of your
  choice, about 300g/10½oz total weight
salt and freshly ground black pepper

SERVES 4 | PREPARATION TIME 30 minutes | COOKING TIME 20 minutes

RÖSTIS WITH HONEY-ROASTED HAM & TOMATOES

Röstis with a well-cooked, crisp outer and a soft potato centre are your goal. If this is
achieved, I can guarantee the whole dish will sing sweetly when devoured! If you want
to make one large rösti, use a 30cm/12in frying pan and cook for about 15 minutes on
each side until golden.

1] Put the potatoes and onion into a large colander. Toss with the salt and leave to drain
for 30 minutes. Transfer to a clean tea towel. Bring the edges of the tea towel together
and twist tightly, squeezing out as much water from the potato mixture as possible.
Transfer to a large bowl, then mix in the flour and season with a little pepper.

2] Preheat the oven to 220°C/425°F/Gas 7. Line a baking sheet with kitchen paper.

3] Heat a thin layer of vegetable oil in a large frying pan over a medium heat. Put a quarter
of the potato mixture in the pan and spread it out to a thin round, about 15cm/6in
in diameter. Repeat to cook two at a time. Fry the röstis for 4–5 minutes on each side
until golden and crisp. Turn the heat down slightly if the outside is browning too
quickly. Transfer to the lined baking sheet and cover with foil to keep warm while you
cook the remaining röstis.

4] While the röstis are cooking, put the tomatoes on a baking tray, drizzle with the olive oil
and sprinkle the sugar over. Season with a little salt and pepper. Roast the tomatoes for
8–10 minutes until softened and the skins just start to split.

5] Serve the röstis topped with a slice of ham and the roasted tomatoes.

300g/10½oz small waxy potatoes, such as Ratte, Charlotte or Pink Fir Apple

30g/1oz unsalted butter, plus extra for greasing

1 bunch of spring onions, thinly sliced

250g/9oz good-quality ham, cut into bite-sized pieces

125g/4½oz cooked, peeled large prawns

100g/3½oz feta cheese, crumbled

6 eggs

4 tbsp double cream

2 tbsp chopped dill

salt and freshly ground black pepper

green salad, to serve

SERVES 4–6 | **PREPARATION TIME** 15 minutes | **COOKING TIME** 1 hour

HAM, PRAWN & FETA FRITTATA

A well-made, flavoursome frittata that makes a satisfying lunchtime meal.

1] Put the potatoes in a large saucepan of cold salted water. Bring to the boil, then turn the heat down and cook for 15–20 minutes until just tender. Drain the potatoes and spread them out on a baking sheet to cool to room temperature.

2] Meanwhile, preheat the oven to 180°C/350°F/Gas 4. Cut a circle of baking paper about 30cm/12in in diameter. Grease the base and side of an ovenproof medium-sized frying pan or skillet with an ovenproof handle. Press the baking paper into the base of the pan and up the sides; the butter should help it to stick. Lining the frying pan will mean that your frittata will turn out cleanly without sticking to the pan.

3] Cut the potatoes into 1cm/½in thick slices. Melt the butter in a separate large frying pan over a high heat. When it is foaming, add the potatoes and fry for 4 minutes, turning occasionally, until golden. Add the spring onions and cook for 1 minute, then remove from the heat and spread the potato mixture over the baking paper in the frying pan. Scatter the ham, prawns and feta over the potatoes, pressing them down slightly.

4] Whisk the eggs, cream and dill together in a jug. Season with a pinch of salt and plenty of pepper. Pour the egg mixture into the pan, shaking it slightly to distribute the egg evenly. Bake the frittata for 25–30 minutes, turning the pan halfway through, until the frittata has just set in the centre.

5] Remove the pan from the oven and turn the frittata out. The easiest way to do this is to put a large heatproof plate or board over the top of the frying pan, then flip it over so that the frittata drops out onto the plate. Take care as the pan will be very hot. Peel the baking paper off immediately to prevent the frittata becoming soggy. Serve hot or cold, cut into wedges and with a green salad.

vegetable oil, for greasing

4 ham steaks, preferably smoked, each about 220g/7oz

30g/1oz unsalted butter

1 tbsp sugar

2 large firm eating apples, preferably Pink Lady, peeled, cored and each cut into 6 wedges

4 handfuls of watercress

1 recipe quantity Creamy Garlic Potatoes (see page 216), to serve

SERVES 4 | **PREPARATION TIME** 10 minutes | **COOKING TIME** 15 minutes

HAM STEAKS WITH CARAMELIZED APPLES

Streets away from the traditional gammon and pineapple, this simple dish is great to eat at any time of the day, from a light lunch to a late supper.

1] Preheat the oven to its lowest setting. Heat a griddle or frying pan over a medium heat and brush with a little oil. Cook the ham steaks for 3–4 minutes on each side until cooked. Transfer the steaks to the oven to keep warm while you cook the apples.

2] Put a medium-sized frying pan over a low heat. Add the butter and sugar and when melted, turn the heat up to high and bubble for 1 minute. Add the apples and cook for 4–5 minutes, turning halfway, until the caramel starts to turn dark amber and is smoking slightly. Take the pan off the heat and keep turning the apples in the caramel for 2 minutes.

3] Spoon the caramelized apple slices and sauce over the ham steaks and serve with a handful of watercress and creamy garlic potatoes.

JOHNNIE'S TIP

If your ham steaks come with a rind, snip the fat at 5mm/¼in intervals using kitchen scissors to prevent the steaks curling up during cooking.

HOW TO CURE BACON

Although bacon is a firm favourite with many people, much of the mass-market produce falls far short of its potential owing to the curing process. Curing may sound complicated but it really isn't – it's just a simple process of preserving meat using salt. Low-grade bacon comes from curing in a salty solution or brine, which results in a lot of excess water in the meat, leaving it flabby and tasteless.

The best method is to dry-cure bacon, using a simple mix of salt and spices. This draws the water out of the pork and leaves only the quality meat and fat, resulting in tastier bacon and one that will crisp up nicely when cooked. Regular sea salt is perfectly effective for the curing process, and pork belly is the easiest as it is a manageable size and shape – also it will only take about 1 week to cure at home.

1kg/2lb 4oz pork belly, skin on
150g/5^{1}/$_{2}$oz/^{1}/$_{2}$ cup coarse sea salt
4 juniper berries, crushed

2 tbsp soft light brown sugar
2 tbsp maple syrup

SERVES 8 | **PREPARATION TIME** 20 minutes, plus 5 days curing and at least 24 hours drying

HOME-CURED BACON WITH MAPLE & JUNIPER

1] Put the pork belly on a chopping board and pat it dry with kitchen paper. Mix together the salt, juniper berries, sugar and maple syrup and rub this all over the pork, making sure you get into any crevices in the meat. Transfer the meat to a heavy-duty resealable freezer bag and add any salt mixture left on the chopping board. Squeeze as much air as possible out of the bag and seal it tightly.

2] Put the bag into a non-metallic dish, so that the meat is sitting skin-side up, and put it in the bottom of the fridge. Leave for 5 days, turning the bag over once a day.

3] After 5 days, take the bacon out of the bag and rinse thoroughly in cold water. Pat dry with kitchen paper and place on a wire rack to dry, uncovered, in a cool place for at least 24 hours (or leave it for a couple of days, if you prefer). The fridge is too humid, so try to find a cool garage or other cool, dry place to let it dry. You can cover the bacon with a piece of muslin while it is drying, as this allows the air to circulate. Slice the bacon thinly before cooking.

"SHOW ME HOW" TO CURE THE BACON

30g/1oz unsalted butter
1 large onion, thinly sliced
1 garlic clove, crushed
200g/7oz lardons, cubetti di pancetta or diced
  smoked streaky bacon
300g/10¹/₂oz baby button mushrooms

125ml/4fl oz/¹/₂ cup dry white wine
185ml/6fl oz/³/₄ cup double cream
100g/3¹/₂oz Emmenthal cheese, grated
salt and freshly ground black pepper
boiled new potatoes or crusty bread and
  crisp green salad, to serve

SERVES 4 | PREPARATION TIME 10 minutes | COOKING TIME 40 minutes

LARDON & MUSHROOM GRATIN

Ian Boasman, former owner of *Bistro French* in Preston, Lancashire, taught me how to cook this cracking little dish; he used to call it "Magic Mushrooms" on his menu!

1] Melt half the butter in a large frying pan over a low heat. Add the onion and garlic and cook for 10–15 minutes, stirring occasionally, until softened and just starting to colour.

2] Meanwhile, put the lardons in a medium-sized saucepan and just cover with cold water. Bring up to simmering point over a medium heat, then drain and repeat this process. Drain again and leave the lardons in a sieve until needed.

3] Using a slotted spoon, scoop the onion and garlic onto a plate and leave to one side. Add the lardons to the frying pan and cook over a medium heat for 5–6 minutes until crisp. Transfer to a bowl.

4] Melt the remaining butter in the frying pan and, when foaming, cook the mushrooms for 8–10 minutes until golden brown. Return the onion and garlic to the pan and tip in the wine. Bring to the boil and cook until the wine has reduced down to a syrupy liquid. Add the cream and boil again for 2–3 minutes until thickened – it should leave a slight ribbon trail when you lift a spoon out of the sauce.

5] Meanwhile, preheat the grill to high. Remove the pan from the heat and stir in the lardons, then season to taste with salt and pepper. Tip the creamy mixture into a flameproof dish, or 4 individual gratin dishes, and sprinkle over the Emmenthal. Grill the gratin for 3 minutes or until the cheese has melted and is bubbling and tinged with brown in places. Serve immediately with new potatoes or crusty bread and a salad.

JOHNNIE'S TIP

If the lardons are smoked, I prefer to blanch them first to reduce their saltiness (see page 30), but you could use a mild-cured, unsmoked pork belly instead. Cut the pork into lardons, omit the blanching, then cook before the onion until crisp. Remove from the pan, then cook the onion in the pork fat left in the pan.

200g/7oz lardons, cubetti di pancetta or diced
   smoked streaky bacon
1 red onion, very finely chopped
1 red pepper, deseeded and very finely diced
1 courgette, very finely diced
2 small red dried chillies, thinly sliced, or
   ½ tsp crushed dried chillies
250ml/9fl oz/1 cup Passata (see page 212)

400g/14oz dried ridged pasta, such as
   penne rigate, rigatoni or lumaconi
30g/1oz Parmesan cheese, finely grated,
   plus extra to serve
1 small handful of flat-leaf parsley leaves,
   finely chopped
salt and freshly ground black pepper
green salad, to serve

SERVES 4 | **PREPARATION TIME** 15 minutes | **COOKING TIME** 35 minutes

PASTA AMATRICIANA

I like to add finely diced vegetables to this spicy amatriciana sauce. They are fried until golden and almost caramelized, so they add an extra dimension to the spicy, smoky sauce. The ridges on the pasta help the sauce cling to it, so every mouthful is packed with flavour.

1] Put the lardons in a large, deep frying pan over a low heat. Cook for 8–10 minutes until the fat melts out of the lardons. Turn the heat up to medium and cook for about 5 minutes until the lardons are crisp. Using a slotted spoon, scoop the lardons onto a plate, leaving the fat in the pan.

2] Add the vegetables to the frying pan and fry over a medium heat for 10–15 minutes, stirring frequently, until they are browned at the edges. Take care towards the end of the cooking time as they can burn easily. Add the chillies and cook for 1 minute, then stir in the passata. Bring to the boil, then turn the heat down and simmer gently for 2 minutes.

3] Meanwhile, cook the pasta in a large pan of boiling salted water for 12 minutes or until al dente. Drain, reserving 250ml/9fl oz/1 cup of the cooking water. Add the cooked pasta to the frying pan and toss it in the sauce, adding a few splashes of the pasta cooking water if the sauce is too thick; it should lightly coat the pasta. Scatter the Parmesan over and season with salt and pepper. Sprinkle the pasta with the parsley and serve with extra Parmesan and a green salad.

150g/5½oz sliced Parma ham
600ml/21fl oz/scant 2½ cups dry white wine
1 bay leaf
1 star anise
6 black peppercorns
250g/9oz asparagus, trimmed
75g/2½oz unsalted butter
2 shallots, very finely chopped

½ celery stalk, strings removed and
   very finely diced
300g/10½oz/1½ cups risotto rice,
   such as Arborio
1 tbsp drained small capers
100g/3½oz Grana Padano cheese,
   finely grated, plus extra to serve
salt and freshly ground black pepper

SERVES 4 | **PREPARATION TIME** 15 minutes | **COOKING TIME** 40 minutes

PARMA HAM & ASPARAGUS RISOTTO

If asparagus is out of season, please avoid force grown or any other form and use calabrese, long-stem or purple-sprouting broccoli instead.

1] Put the Parma ham into a large, dry frying pan and set over a low heat. Cook the ham for 3–4 minutes, turning once, until crisp. Reserve 4 slices of the ham and break the remainder into small pieces, then leave to one side.

2] Put the wine in a medium-sized saucepan with the bay leaf, star anise and peppercorns. Add 600ml/21fl oz/scant 2½ cups water and bring to the boil over a high heat. Turn the heat down to very low and keep the wine mixture warm.

3] Cut off the tips of the asparagus and leave them to one side. Cut the stalks into very fine dice. Melt 60g/2¼oz of the butter in a large saucepan. Add the shallots, celery and diced asparagus stalks and cook very gently for 10 minutes until the vegetables have softened.

4] Add the rice and cook for 3–4 minutes, stirring, until the grains are slightly translucent around the edges. Add a small ladleful of the wine mixture and simmer, stirring continuously, until the liquid has been absorbed. Continue adding ladlefuls of the wine mixture, stirring, until the rice is tender but still has a slight "bite" to it; this should take about 17–20 minutes and you may not need all of the wine mixture. Remove the risotto from the heat and leave it to stand, covered, for 2 minutes.

5] Meanwhile, cook the asparagus tips in boiling salted water for 2 minutes or until just tender.

6] Stir the remaining butter into the risotto with the capers and Grana Padano. Fold in the Parma ham pieces. Season with salt and pepper, to taste, and add a little extra liquid if needed – the rice should be soft but still hold its shape. Serve the risotto topped with the asparagus tips, reserved Parma ham and sprinkled with extra Grana Padano.

1 tbsp olive oil
1 onion, finely chopped
3 garlic cloves, crushed
250g/9oz/1⅓ cups Puy lentils, rinsed
125ml/4fl oz/½ cup dry white wine
375ml/13fl oz/1½ cups vegetable stock
1 long rosemary sprig, needles finely chopped
1 bay leaf

a pinch of crushed dried chillies
2 tbsp vegetable oil
450g/1lb spicy sausages, about 8 in total, such
   as Italian-style sausages, or cooking chorizo
   sausages
1 handful of flat-leaf parsley leaves, chopped
salt and freshly ground black pepper
crusty bread and rocket salad, to serve

SERVES 4 | **PREPARATION TIME** 10 minutes | **COOKING TIME** 45 minutes

SPICY SAUSAGE WITH LENTILS

Spicy sausages pair very well with the nutty, earthy flavour of Puy lentils to give a hearty, warming dish. Any leftovers are also good tossed with a little olive oil and lemon juice to make a lunchtime salad. Remember that good-quality sausages are a must.

1] Put the olive oil in a large saucepan over a low heat. Add the onion and garlic and cook for 8–10 minutes, stirring occasionally, until softened. Add the lentils, white wine, stock, rosemary, bay leaf and chillies. Increase the heat to medium-high and bring the liquid to the boil. Boil the lentils for 5 minutes, then turn the heat down, cover the pan and simmer for 20–25 minutes until the liquid has been absorbed and the lentils are tender.

2] Meanwhile, put the vegetable oil in a large frying pan over a medium heat. When the oil is shimmering, add the sausages and cook for 15 minutes, turning regularly, until browned all over and cooked through. Leave the pan to one side until the lentils are ready.

3] Uncover the lentils and season with salt and pepper. Tip the lentils into the sausage pan and stir until combined. Warm over a low heat for 2 minutes, then remove from the heat and scatter the parsley over the top. Serve with crusty bread and a rocket salad.

CURED, DRIED, PRESERVED & SMOKED

500g/1lb 2oz pork tenderloin fillet, fat and
    silverskin membrane trimmed, cut into
    8 equal pieces
16 slices of Parma ham or prosciutto crudo
8 sage leaves
55g/2oz unsalted butter
1 tsp vegetable oil

2 tbsp dry white wine
1 tbsp drained small capers
freshly ground black pepper
1 recipe quantity Green Beans with Garlic
    & Almonds (see page 218) or other green
    vegetable, such as peas, to serve

SERVES 4 | **PREPARATION TIME** 20 minutes | **COOKING TIME** 15 minutes

PORK SALTIMBOCCA

This variation on the veal classic is one of my favourite dishes, and it's simple, quick and very tasty.

1] Preheat the oven to 70°C/150°F/Gas ¼. Put the pork pieces on a large chopping board, then cover with cling film and beat with a meat mallet or rolling pin until 2mm/¹⁄₁₆in thick. Season each piece with a little pepper.

2] Lay 2 slices of the Parma ham, slightly overlapping, on a clean chopping board or large plate and put a sage leaf in the centre. Sit a piece of pork on top. Wrap the ham around the pork to make a parcel; the ham should stick to itself but you can secure it with a wooden cocktail stick, if necessary. Repeat to make 8 parcels in total.

3] Heat the butter and oil in a large frying pan over a medium-high heat. When the butter is foaming, add the pork parcels and cook for 2–3 minutes on each side until the ham is crisp. You may need to cook them in two batches. Transfer the saltimbocca to a low oven to keep warm.

4] Add the wine to the pan. Leave it to bubble for 1 minute, then remove the pan from the heat and stir in the capers. Spoon the sauce and capers over the saltimbocca and serve with the green beans with garlic and almonds or other green vegetable.

10g/¼oz/⅓ cup dried porcini mushrooms

30g/1oz unsalted butter

2 shallots, very finely chopped

1 garlic clove, crushed

250g/9oz chestnut mushrooms, thinly sliced

2 thyme sprigs, leaves removed

4 tbsp Marsala

100g/3½oz/½ cup good-quality black olives, pitted and finely chopped

500g/1lb 2oz pork tenderloin fillet, fat and silverskin membrane trimmed

125g/4½oz sliced pancetta or dry-cured smoked streaky bacon

2 tbsp vegetable oil

salt and freshly ground black pepper

1 recipe quantity Savoy Cabbage with Lardons (see page 219), boiled new potatoes and lemon wedges, to serve

SERVES 4 | PREPARATION TIME 40 minutes, plus soaking | COOKING TIME 45 minutes

PANCETTA-WRAPPED PORK WITH MUSHROOM STUFFING

1] Put the porcini in a bowl and cover with just-boiled water. Leave to soak for 30 minutes until softened. Strain, reserving the soaking liquid, and roughly chop the mushrooms.

2] Melt the butter in a large frying pan over a low heat. Add the shallots and garlic and cook for 8–10 minutes, stirring occasionally until softened. Increase the heat to medium-high, add the chestnut mushrooms and thyme and cook for about 10 minutes, stirring frequently, until the mushrooms have softened.

3] Add the porcini and cook for 1 minute, then pour in the Marsala and mushroom soaking liquid and bring to the boil. Cook until the liquid has evaporated but the stuffing is still moist. Remove from the heat, stir in the olives and season with salt and pepper to taste. Leave to cool slightly.

4] Preheat the oven to 200°C/400°F/Gas 6. Make a horizontal cut along the centre of the pork, not quite slicing it all the way through. Open out the fillet like a book, cover with cling film, and beat with a meat mallet or rolling pin until the meat is 3mm/⅛in thick; try to keep the meat in a rectangular shape. Season with salt and pepper.

5] Lay the pancetta slices vertically on a sheet of baking paper, slightly overlapping them; you need to make a bed of pancetta slightly longer than the pork fillet. Spread the mushroom filling down one side of the pork and fold it over to encase the filling. Lay the fillet horizontally on top of the pancetta and, using the baking paper to help you, roll the pancetta around the pork. You can tie it with string to secure, if you like.

6] Heat the oil in a large frying pan over a medium heat. Brown the pork for 10 minutes, turning until golden all over. Transfer to a roasting tin and roast for 12 minutes. Remove from the oven, rest the pork for 10 minutes, then cut into 8 slices. Serve with the Savoy cabbage with lardons, new potatoes and lemon wedges.

"SHOW ME HOW" TO WRAP THE TENDERLOIN

CHAPTER 3

SPICY &
AROMATIC

Pork and spices were almost made for each other. The mild flavour of pork is a great canvas for spices – in fact, the meat benefits from the extra flavour.

It may come as little surprise to discover that pork is one of Asia's favourite meats, and chilli-hot dishes such as Pork Sichuan Noodles and Korean-style Fiery Pork show how perfect pork is for Asian-style cooking. But it's not all about heat, so for a milder spicy option, try the sweet-savoury tang of Teriyaki Pork Skewers with Pickled Vegetables or Pork Dim Sum, which are both fun to make and eat.

Asian cooking doesn't have a monopoly on superbly spiced dishes, and there is plenty of inspiration in this chapter from Latin American countries, including South American-style Spicy Pork Pasties, Hot Mexican Pork Burgers and Green Pork Chilli Tacos. The Caribbean, too, is represented with a taste bud-tingling Jerk Pork served with a cooling Mango Salsa, while there is also the popular American Spicy Pork Meatloaf.

Even the Europeans like to spice pork up. Look for the delicious Spanish Pork Skewers, or why not try making *pimentón*-spiked Fresh Chorizo Sausages? Whatever your mood or preference, there is a dish to tempt you.

450g/1lb pork tenderloin fillet, fat and silverskin membrane trimmed, cut into 1cm/¼in thick slices

3 garlic cloves, crushed

1 lemongrass stalk, tough outer leaves removed, very finely chopped

3 tbsp fish sauce

3 tbsp soft light brown sugar

vegetable oil, for greasing

1 or 2 baguettes, cut into 4 pieces about 15cm/6in long

100ml/3½fl oz mayonnaise

2 fresh red chillies, deseeded and thinly sliced

1 large handful of coriander leaves

½ cucumber, deseeded and cut into matchsticks

PICKLED VEGETABLES

1 carrot, cut into matchsticks

12cm/4½in piece daikon (mooli), peeled and cut into matchsticks

½ tsp salt

150ml/5fl oz/scant ⅔ cup rice wine vinegar

4 tbsp caster sugar

SERVES 4 | **PREPARATION TIME** 45 minutes, plus marinating | **COOKING TIME** 15 minutes

VIETNAMESE BAGUETTE

Called *Banh mi* in Vietnam, this is a sandwich that is usually filled with pork and pickled vegetables. I like to use a marinated pork fillet.

1] To make the pickled vegetables, put the carrot and daikon in a colander and toss with the salt; leave to one side for 20 minutes until softened, then rinse and pat dry with kitchen paper. In a bowl, mix together the vinegar, caster sugar and 125ml/4fl oz/½ cup warm water until the sugar dissolves. Add the vegetables and marinate for 1 hour, or store in the fridge until needed. (The vegetables will keep in the fridge for up to 1 week.)

2] Meanwhile, cover the pork slices with cling film, then beat with a meat mallet or rolling pin until about 3mm/⅛in thick.

3] Mix together the garlic, lemongrass, fish sauce and soft light brown sugar in a large bowl. Add the pork and turn to coat, then leave to marinate for 30 minutes.

4] Heat a griddle or large frying pan over a high heat until it is smoking hot. Brush with a little vegetable oil, then cook the marinated pork for 2–3 minutes on each side. Don't overcrowd the pan, and you may need to cook the pork in batches. Transfer the cooked meat to a plate and let the pork cool slightly.

5] Cut each portion of baguette in half lengthways and hollow out the top section slightly to make room for the filling. Spread a little mayonnaise over the base and scatter over the chillies. Sit the pork slices on top, then add the coriander and cucumber. Drain the pickled vegetables and spoon them on top, sandwich everything together, then serve.

1l/35fl oz/4 cups vegetable stock

4 fresh bird's eye chillies, roughly chopped

3 garlic cloves, thinly sliced

3 lemongrass stalks, tough outer leaves removed, roughly chopped

2.5cm/1in piece fresh ginger, thinly sliced (no need to peel)

10 coriander sprigs

2 kaffir lime leaves, or 3 long strips of pared lime rind

100g/3½oz dried vermicelli rice noodles

½ tsp fish sauce

juice of ½ lime

1 tbsp soft light brown sugar

300g/10½oz pork loin steaks, fat trimmed, cut into 3mm/⅛in cubes

100g/3½oz small oriental mushrooms, such as enoki or shimenji

150g/5½oz small cooked peeled prawns

fish sauce, thinly sliced fresh bird's eye chillies, lime wedges and 1 handful each of coriander leaves and Thai basil leaves (optional), to serve

SERVES 4 | **PREPARATION TIME** 25 minutes | **COOKING TIME** 40 minutes

HOT & SOUR NOODLE SOUP WITH PORK

I like to serve my hot and sour soup truly Thai-style, with each person helping themselves to extra fish sauce, chopped chillies, lime juice and fresh coriander, according to their own taste. Top each serving with a few Thai basil leaves, too, if available.

1] Put the vegetable stock in a large saucepan with the chillies, garlic, lemongrass, ginger, coriander sprigs and kaffir lime leaves. Add 250ml/9fl oz/1 cup water. Bring to the boil over a high heat, then turn the heat down to low and simmer for 30 minutes.

2] Meanwhile, put the noodles into a large bowl and cover with warm water. Leave to soak for 20 minutes until the noodles have just softened, then drain and leave to one side.

3] Strain the aromatic stock into a clean saucepan and stir in the fish sauce, lime juice and sugar. Return to the boil over a high heat, then turn the heat down to low and add the pork, mushrooms and drained noodles. Simmer for 2–3 minutes until the mushrooms have softened. Add the prawns and cook for another 1 minute until warmed through.

4] Serve the soup, helping yourself to the extra fish sauce, chillies, lime wedges, coriander and basil, if using.

1 tbsp vegetable oil, plus extra for deep frying
½ small onion, finely chopped
½ red pepper, deseeded and finely diced
1 garlic clove, crushed
½ tsp ground cumin
½ tsp paprika
½ tsp cayenne pepper
200g/7oz pork mince
3 tbsp white wine or dry sherry
2 tbsp raisins, finely chopped
6 pimento-stuffed green olives, finely chopped
salt and freshly ground black pepper

DOUGH

300g/10½oz/scant 2½ cups plain
  flour, plus extra for dusting
2 tsp baking powder
½ tsp salt
30g/1oz lard
125ml/4fl oz/½ cup milk
1 egg

SERVES 4–8 (makes 16) | **PREPARATION TIME** 45 minutes, plus cooling and chilling | **COOKING TIME** 45 minutes

SOUTH AMERICAN-STYLE SPICY PORK PASTIES

These are wonderful for a picnic, dipped into a sweet-and-spicy sauce or mayonnaise.

1] Put the 1 tablespoon of oil in a large frying pan over a medium heat. Add the onion, pepper and garlic and cook for 8–10 minutes until softened. Add the cumin, paprika and cayenne and cook for 2 minutes, then transfer to a bowl. Turn the heat up to high.

2] Add the mince and cook, breaking it up with a spoon, for 6–8 minutes until browned. Return the onion mixture to the pan, add the wine and 3 tablespoons water. Bring to the boil and cook for 4–5 minutes until the liquid has evaporated. Remove from the heat and stir in the raisins and olives. Season and leave to one side to cool completely.

3] To make the dough, sift the flour, baking powder and salt into a bowl. Rub the lard into the flour until you can no longer see any lumps of fat. Whisk together the milk and egg and add to the flour mixture, a little at a time, to make a soft dough. Form the dough into a disc, wrap in cling film and put in the fridge for 1 hour.

4] Dust a work surface with flour, then roll out the dough and cut out 16 circles, roughly 10cm/4in in diameter. Put 1 heaped tablespoon of the filling on one side of a circle of dough. Dampen the edge of the dough with water, then fold it over to make a half-moon shape and crimp with your fingers or a fork to seal. Repeat to make 16 in total.

5] Pour enough oil into a large saucepan to fill by one-third and heat to 180°C/350°. Fry the pasties for 4 minutes, turning occasionally, until golden. You will need to cook them in batches of 3 or 4 and bring the oil back up to heat before adding a new batch. Transfer the pasties to a baking tray lined with kitchen paper and cool slightly before serving.

"SHOW ME HOW" TO FILL AND FRY THE PASTIES

175g/6oz pork loin steak, fat trimmed,
   cut into cubes
110g/3¾oz small cooked peeled prawns,
   patted dry
8 water chestnuts, roughly chopped
6 spring onions, finely chopped
4cm/1½in piece fresh ginger, peeled
   and grated
5 tsp oyster sauce
2 tsp soy sauce
1½ tsp sugar

28 wonton wrappers
chives, to serve

DIPPING SAUCE
4 tbsp soy sauce
2 tbsp rice wine vinegar
4 tbsp soft light brown sugar
2 tsp toasted sesame oil
2 small spring onions, thinly sliced
½ fresh red chilli, deseeded and diced

SERVES 4 (makes about 28) | **PREPARATION TIME** 40 minutes | **COOKING TIME** 25 minutes

PORK DIM SUM

These steamed dim sum dumplings resemble moneybags. Serve them as a starter, followed by a stir-fry and some rice. Sweet chilli sauce would be a good alternative to the dipping sauce.

1] Finely chop the pork in a food processor for 1–2 minutes. Add the prawns and pulse about 6–8 times until chopped, then add the water chestnuts and spring onions and pulse 4–6 times until combined. Transfer to a bowl and stir in the ginger, oyster and soy sauces and sugar.

2] Lay a wonton wrapper on a chopping board. Put a slightly heaped teaspoonful of the pork mixture in the centre and brush around the filling with water. Bring the corners of the wonton wrapper together, squeeze and twist the top to seal and to make a "moneybag". Transfer to a baking sheet lined with cling film and keep covered with more cling film to prevent it drying out. Keep the unused wonton wrappers covered as well. Repeat with the remaining wrappers and pork mixture until they are all used up.

3] Line a large bamboo steamer with baking paper. Put the dumplings in the steamer, making sure they don't touch each other, cover and steam over a wok or saucepan of boiling water for 6–8 minutes. You may need to cook the dumplings in a tiered steamer or in batches.

4] To make the dipping sauce, mix together the soy sauce, vinegar, sugar and sesame oil with 4 tablespoons water. Divide into 4 small dipping bowls and scatter a little spring onion and chilli on top.

5] Scatter a few chives over the dim sum and serve with the dipping sauce.

"SHOW ME HOW" TO FILL AND FORM THE DIM SUM

100g/3½oz dried rice vermicelli noodles

3 tbsp fish sauce

3 tbsp lime juice

2 tbsp soft light brown sugar

4 pork loin steaks, each about 175g/6oz, fat trimmed

4 fresh green bird's eye chillies, thinly sliced

55g/2oz/⅓ cup shelled unsalted peanuts

1 tbsp vegetable oil

1 cucumber, deseeded and cut into matchsticks

1 large carrot, cut into matchsticks

10 radishes, thinly sliced

½ red pepper, deseeded and thinly sliced

2 tomatoes, deseeded and thinly sliced

2 handfuls of beansprouts

1 large handful of mint leaves

1 large handful of coriander leaves

SERVES 4 | **PREPARATION TIME** 40 minutes, plus soaking and chilling (optional) | **COOKING TIME** 20 minutes

VIETNAMESE PORK SALAD

Pork is probably the most popular meat in Vietnam and it is prepared in a variety of ways. Fried until golden and served as part of a summery noodle salad, as here, is one of the best.

1] Put the noodles into a large bowl and cover with just-boiled water. Leave to one side for 20 minutes until the noodles have softened, then drain, rinse with cold water and drain again. Chill the noodles for 4 hours before using, if possible.

2] Whisk together the fish sauce, lime juice and sugar until the sugar dissolves. Rub 1 tablespoon of the mixture over the pork steaks and leave them to stand for 10 minutes. Add the chillies to the remaining fish sauce dressing and leave to one side.

3] Toast the peanuts for 3–4 minutes in a large, dry frying pan over a medium heat, tossing the pan frequently. Transfer the peanuts to a plate to cool, then chop or crush roughly.

4] Add the oil to the pan and cook the pork steaks for around 3 minutes on each side until browned on the outside and just pink in the centre. Don't overcrowd the pan – you may need to cook the pork in two batches. Cover the pork and leave it to rest for 5 minutes.

5] Put the drained noodles into a serving bowl with the cucumber, carrot, radishes, pepper, tomatoes, beansprouts, mint and coriander. Add the dressing and toss together. Slice the pork steaks thinly. Serve the noodle salad topped with the pork strips and peanuts.

450g/1lb pork loin steaks, fat trimmed,
  cut into 1cm/½in cubes
¼ cucumber, deseeded and cubed
8 small spring onions, halved
steamed jasmine rice, to serve (optional)

MARINADE
4 tbsp coconut milk
1 tbsp soy sauce
1 tbsp soft light brown sugar
1 tbsp vegetable oil
1 lemongrass stalk, tough outer leaves
  removed, very finely chopped
6 cardamom pods, seeds crushed and pods
  discarded
1cm/½in piece fresh ginger, peeled and grated
1 tsp garam masala

½ tsp turmeric
1 garlic clove, crushed
freshly ground black pepper

SATAY SAUCE
1 tbsp vegetable oil
2 shallots, very finely chopped
½ tsp garam masala
½cm/¼in piece fresh ginger, peeled and
  grated
1 fresh red chilli, deseeded and finely chopped
50g/2oz/¾ cup finely grated fresh coconut
5 tbsp coconut milk
2 tsp soy sauce
2 tsp lime juice
1 tsp soft light brown sugar

SERVES 4 (makes 16) | **PREPARATION TIME** 30 minutes, plus overnight marinating |
COOKING TIME 15 minutes

MAURITIAN PORK SATAY

**Thai pork satay with peanut sauce is familiar to most people, yet in Mauritius they make
a creamy coconut version that is slightly less fiery, but still aromatic and delicious.**

1] Put the pork into a non-metallic bowl. Mix together the marinade ingredients with a
generous grinding of pepper, then pour it over the pork and toss to coat. Cover and
marinate in the fridge for 8 hours, or overnight.

2] Meanwhile, to make the satay sauce, put the oil in a medium-sized saucepan over a
medium heat. Add the shallots and cook for 5–6 minutes until softened. Add the garam
masala and ginger and cook for 1 minute, then remove from the heat and leave to cool.
Stir in the remaining ingredients and refrigerate until needed. Thirty minutes before you
are ready to cook, soak 16 wooden skewers in warm water to prevent them burning.

3] Preheat the grill to high and line the grill pan with foil. Thread the cubes of pork onto
the skewers, then grill for 3–4 minutes on each side until slightly charred and just cooked.

4] Put the cucumber and spring onions in the centre of a serving platter and arrange the
skewers around the edge. Give the satay sauce a stir and divide it into 4 small bowls.
Serve the satay so that each person can add a little cucumber and spring onion to their
skewers, then dip them in the sauce to eat. Serve with jasmine rice, if you like.

700g/1lb 9oz pork loin steaks, fat trimmed, cut into 1cm/½in cubes

½ onion, very finely chopped

2 garlic cloves, crushed

2 tbsp olive oil

1½ tsp hot smoked paprika

½ tsp ground cumin

½ tsp ground coriander

½ tsp dried oregano

¼ tsp black pepper

salt

crusty bread and lemon wedges, to serve

SERVES 4 (makes 16) | **PREPARATION TIME** 30 minutes, plus overnight marinating | **COOKING TIME** 10 minutes

SPANISH PORK SKEWERS

Pinchos morunos, **meaning "Moorish skewers", is a popular tapas dish offered in bars all over Spain. It can be served as part of a tapas platter with some thinly sliced Hot-smoked Pork Tenderloin (see page 82), small bowls of Chorizo Rancheros, without the eggs (see page 74) and thinly sliced manchego cheese. Fantastic!**

1] Put the pork into a bowl and scatter the onion over. Mix together the garlic, oil, paprika, cumin, coriander, oregano and pepper. Spoon it over the pork and onion, then turn until coated. Cover and leave to marinate in the fridge for 8 hours, or overnight.

2] Meanwhile, soak 16 wooden skewers in warm water for at least 30 minutes to prevent them burning.

3] Preheat the grill to high and line the grill pan with foil. Remove the pork from the marinade and thread the cubes of pork onto the skewers. Brush with a little of the marinade left in the bowl and season each skewer with a little salt. Grill for 3–4 minutes on each side until the pork is slightly charred and just cooked.

4] Serve the skewers hot or at room temperature with crusty bread and lemon wedges.

4 pork leg steaks, about 600g/1lb 5oz total weight

TERIYAKI SAUCE
125ml/4fl oz/½ cup mirin
125ml/4fl oz/½ cup soy sauce
4 tbsp sake or dry sherry
3 tbsp soft light brown sugar

PICKLED VEGETABLES
125ml/4fl oz/½ cup rice vinegar
5 tsp sugar
¼ tsp salt
1 small piece kombu seaweed (optional)
½ cucumber, peeled, deseeded and cut into matchsticks
2 carrots, cut into matchsticks

SERVES 4 | PREPARATION TIME 2½ hours | COOKING TIME 10 minutes

TERIYAKI PORK SKEWERS WITH PICKLED VEGETABLES

1] To make the pickled vegetables, mix together the vinegar, sugar, salt and kombu, if using, in a non-metallic bowl with 4 tablespoons just-boiled water. Add the cucumber and carrots and toss to coat them in the liquid, then leave to one side for 1–2 hours.

2] Meanwhile, to make the sauce, put the mirin, soy sauce, sake and sugar in a medium-sized saucepan over a high heat. Bring to the boil, then turn the heat down and simmer for 20 minutes until reduced by half. Leave to one side for 1 hour to cool.

3] Cover the pork with cling film and beat with a meat mallet or rolling pin until 5mm/¼in thick. Cut each steak into 3 long strips and transfer to a bowl. Pour the teriyaki sauce over, reserving 4 tablespoons to serve, and toss until coated. Leave to marinate for 30 minutes, but not much longer as the pork can become tough and dry if left for too long. Stir the pork every 10 minutes while it is marinating.

4] Preheat the grill to high and line the grill pan with foil. Remove the pork from the teriyaki sauce and thread it onto metal skewers. Brush the pork with some of the sauce and grill for 1 minute. Brush with more of the sauce and grill for 2 more minutes, then turn the skewers over and brush with more sauce. Grill for 1 minute, brush with sauce a final time and grill for a further 2 minutes until just cooked.

5] Drain the pickled vegetables and remove the kombu, if using. Serve the teriyaki pork skewers with the reserved sauce for drizzling over the top and the pickled vegetables.

350g/12oz pork loin steaks, fat trimmed

7 tsp soy sauce

1 tbsp Chinese cooking wine or dry sherry

2 tsp toasted sesame oil

1 tsp sugar

4 tbsp vegetable oil

2 fresh red chillies, deseeded and thinly sliced

3 garlic cloves, 2 thinly sliced and 1 crushed

1 handful of parsley leaves, chopped

4 eggs

2.5cm/1in piece fresh ginger, peeled and grated

6 spring onions, thinly sliced

110g/3¾oz shiitake mushrooms, thinly sliced

1 handful of beansprouts

225g/8oz tinned bamboo shoots, drained and
  cut into matchsticks

20 Mandarin or Chinese pancakes

about 6 tbsp hoisin sauce

SERVES 4 | **PREPARATION TIME** 30 minutes | **COOKING TIME** 20 minutes

STIR-FRY PORK WITH PANCAKES

1] Cover the pork with cling film, then beat with a meat mallet or rolling pin until 3mm/⅛in thick. Cut the pork into little finger-sized pieces and transfer to a bowl. Add 2 tablespoons of the soy sauce, the Chinese cooking wine, sesame oil and sugar. Mix together until the pork is coated and set aside.

2] Heat 1 tablespoon of the oil in a wok or large frying pan over a medium-high heat and stir-fry the chillies, sliced garlic and parsley for 1 minute until starting to colour and turn crisp. Drain on kitchen paper and leave to one side.

3] To make the omelette, whisk the eggs with the remaining soy sauce and 1 tablespoon cold water. Put 1 tablespoon of the oil in the wok or frying pan over a high heat. When the oil is shimmering, pour in the eggs and tilt the pan so they cover the base. Cook the omelette for 1–2 minutes until golden on the bottom and slightly puffed up. Using a spatula, carefully flip the omelette over and cook for a further 1–2 minutes until set. Cut into thin strips and leave to one side.

4] Heat the remaining oil in the wok and add the crushed garlic and ginger. Let them sizzle for 30 seconds, then add the spring onions and mushrooms and stir-fry for 4–5 minutes until softened. Move the vegetables to one side of the wok, tip in the pork and any liquid left in the bowl and stir-fry for 1 minute. Stir the vegetables into the pork and add the beansprouts and bamboo shoots. Stir-fry for a further 2 minutes, then stir in the omelette strips and remove from the heat.

5] Heat the pancakes following the packet instructions. Scatter the reserved parsley mixture over the pork stir-fry. Let everyone help themselves to the pork stir-fry, spooning it on top of the pancakes and then drizzling hoisin sauce over the top. Wrap the pancake around the filling and eat immediately.

450g/1lb pork tenderloin fillet, fat and
  silverskin membrane trimmed, cut into
  2mm/¹⁄₁₆in thick slices
2 garlic cloves, crushed
2cm/³⁄₄in piece fresh ginger, peeled and grated
2 tbsp *gochujang* paste or hot chilli paste
2 tbsp soy sauce

2 tbsp mirin
2 tbsp soft light brown sugar
2 tsp sesame oil
vegetable oil, for greasing
boiled white rice, Hearts of Romaine lettuce
  leaves and kimchi (optional), to serve

SERVES 4 | **PREPARATION TIME** 15 minutes, plus marinating | **COOKING TIME** 15 minutes

KOREAN-STYLE FIERY PORK

The pork must be cut and then beaten into very thin slices and cooked over a very high heat in this classic Korean dish, called *daeji bulgogi*. You will find *gochujang* (Korean hot pepper) paste in Asian grocers or online, but you could use a hot chilli paste. Any leftovers are fantastic as part of a filling for the Vietnamese Baguette (see page 114).

1] Cover the pork slices with cling film, then beat with a meat mallet or rolling pin until very thin, about 2mm/¹⁄₁₆in thick.

2] Mix together the garlic, ginger, *gochujang* paste, soy sauce, mirin, sugar and sesame oil in a large bowl. Add the pork and toss to coat, then leave to marinate for 30 minutes.

3] Heat a griddle or large frying pan over a high heat until it is smoking hot. Brush with a little vegetable oil, then cook the marinated pork for 1–2 minutes on each side until cooked. You will need to do this in batches, pressing the slices of pork onto the ridges of the griddle with a pair of tongs to get the charred lines. Transfer the cooked pork to a warm serving dish and cover with foil while you cook the remaining pork.

4] Serve the pork with the boiled rice, lettuce and the kimchi by the side, if using. Alternatively, serve the pork wrapped in the lettuce leaves with the kimchi.

JOHNNIE'S TIP

It is important to trim the silverskin or white connective tissue surrounding the pork tenderloin as it becomes very tough as it cooks. If the recipe calls for the tenderloin to be cooked whole, it looks better if the ends are trimmed first to neaten the appearance of the fillet. The trimmed ends can be saved and stir-fried or beaten into medallions for another meal.

700g/1lb 9oz pork loin steaks, fat trimmed, cut into bite-sized pieces

4 tbsp cornflour

4 tbsp soy sauce

4 tbsp rice wine or dry sherry

100g/3½oz/scant ⅔ cup shelled unsalted peanuts

2 tbsp vegetable oil

½ tsp crushed dried chillies

2 fresh red chillies, deseeded and thinly sliced

1 lemongrass stalk, tough outer leaves removed, very finely chopped

2.5cm/1in piece fresh ginger, peeled and grated

4 garlic cloves, very thinly sliced

1 tbsp rice wine vinegar

1 tbsp sugar, plus extra to taste

4 spring onions, thinly sliced

1 handful of coriander leaves

steamed jasmine rice, to serve

SERVES 4 | **PREPARATION TIME** 15 minutes, plus marinating | **COOKING TIME** 15 minutes

LEMONGRASS & GINGER STIR-FRY PORK

Stir-fried pork, *kung pao*-style, comes from the Sichuan Province in China, so it is full of bold flavours and very spicy – perfect for anyone who loves chillies, ginger and peanuts.

1] Put the pork into a large bowl and sprinkle the cornflour over, then add the soy sauce and rice wine. Mix everything together and leave to marinate for 30 minutes, then drain the pork, reserving the marinade. Add 125ml/4fl oz/½ cup water to the marinade.

2] Toast the peanuts in a dry wok or large frying pan over a medium heat for 3–4 minutes. Transfer to a plate and leave to one side. Put the oil in the wok over a high heat. When the oil is shimmering, add the dried and fresh chillies, lemongrass, ginger and garlic and sizzle for 1 minute. Add the drained pork and stir-fry for 4–5 minutes until it is just cooked.

3] Add the reserved marinade and bring to the boil, stirring, until the sauce thickens. Add a splash of extra water if it becomes too thick; the sauce should just cling to the meat.

4] Remove from the heat and stir in the peanuts, vinegar and sugar. Taste and add a little extra sugar if you like; you should have a balance of sour and sweet. Scatter the spring onions and coriander over the top, and serve with jasmine rice.

300g/10½oz dried medium egg noodles

2 tsp sesame oil

500g/1lb 2oz pork mince

2 tbsp soft light brown sugar

2 tbsp oyster sauce

2 tbsp vegetable oil

1 tsp Sichuan peppercorns, crushed

½ tsp crushed dried chillies

2.5cm/1in piece fresh ginger, peeled and grated

4 garlic cloves, thinly sliced

1 bunch of spring onions, thinly sliced

4 pak choi, thinly sliced

3 tbsp soy sauce

1 handful of coriander leaves

lime wedges, to serve

SERVES 4 | **PREPARATION TIME** 20 minutes | **COOKING TIME** 25 minutes

PORK SICHUAN NOODLES

Also known as *dan dan* noodles, this stir-fry has a great combination of textures, plus a spicy kick from the Sichuan pepper.

1] Cook the noodles following the instructions on the packet. Drain and toss the noodles in the sesame oil, then leave to one side.

2] Heat a wok or large frying pan over a high heat. Add the pork and stir-fry for about 8–10 minutes until it is browned and crisp in places. Stir in the sugar and oyster sauce, then transfer the mince mixture to a bowl.

3] Return the wok to the heat and add the oil. When the oil is shimmering, add the Sichuan pepper, dried chillies, ginger, garlic and spring onions. Leave them to sizzle for 1 minute, then add the pak choi and stir-fry for 2–3 minutes until wilted.

4] Return the pork to the wok, add the noodles and stir-fry for a further 2–3 minutes until the noodles are heated through. Remove from the heat and stir in the soy sauce. Scatter the coriander over the top and serve with lime wedges.

350g/12oz pork loin steaks, fat trimmed

3 tbsp cornflour

150ml/5fl oz/scant ⅔ cup chicken stock

3 tbsp oyster sauce

2 tbsp soy sauce

2 tbsp dark muscovado sugar

2 tbsp vegetable oil

2.5cm/1in piece fresh ginger, peeled and grated

2 garlic cloves, crushed

1 small onion, thinly sliced

120g/4½oz fresh shiitake mushrooms, tough stalks removed, sliced

100g/3½oz enoki or shimenji mushrooms (or extra shiitake)

100g/3½oz mangetout

150g/5½oz beansprouts

1 tsp sesame oil

225g/8oz tinned water chestnuts, drained and sliced

4 spring onions, thinly sliced

1 red chilli, deseeded and thinly sliced

steamed jasmine rice, to serve

SERVES 4 | **PREPARATION TIME** 30 minutes | **COOKING TIME** 20 minutes

PORK & MUSHROOM STIR-FRY

To avoid overcooking the pork, I stir-fry it separately from the vegetables and add the sauce while the meat is still slightly pink. By the time the sauce has come to the boil, the meat is perfectly cooked.

1] Cover the pork with cling film, then beat with a meat mallet or rolling pin until about 2mm/1⁄16in thick. Cut the pork into little finger-sized pieces and transfer to a bowl. Toss the pork in 2 tablespoons of the cornflour and leave to one side. Mix the remaining cornflour with the stock, oyster and soy sauces and sugar, then leave to one side.

2] Put 1 tablespoon of the oil in a wok or large frying pan over a high heat. When the oil is shimmering, add the ginger and garlic and sizzle for 30 seconds. Add the onion and stir-fry for 3–4 minutes until turning golden at the edges. Next, add the mushrooms and stir-fry for 2–3 minutes until softened, then add the mangetout and stir-fry for 2 minutes. Finally, add the beansprouts and stir-fry for another 1 minute or until softened slightly but still crisp. Transfer the vegetables to a large bowl.

3] Add the remaining oil to the wok and heat again until shimmering. Add the sesame oil and the pork, spread it out in the wok and cook for 1–2 minutes until browned on the underside but still slightly pink on top. Return the vegetables to the wok with the stock mixture and water chestnuts and bring to the boil, stirring, then cook for about 30 seconds until the sauce has thickened. Sprinkle with the spring onions and chilli and serve immediately with jasmine rice.

SPICY & AROMATIC

2 pork tenderloin fillets, each about 450g/1lb,
  fat and silverskin membrane trimmed
baked sweet potatoes, to serve

JERK PASTE
2 fresh Scotch Bonnet chillies, deseeded
  and roughly chopped
2 garlic cloves, roughly chopped
2 tbsp vegetable oil
1 tbsp lime juice
1 tsp ground allspice
1 tsp soy sauce
1 tsp dark muscovado sugar

1cm/½in piece fresh ginger, peeled
  and roughly chopped
¼ tsp ground black pepper
2 thyme sprigs, leaves removed

MANGO SALSA
1 large mango, peeled, pitted and diced
4 spring onions, finely chopped
8 mint leaves, finely chopped
2 tbsp lime juice
2 tsp olive oil
salt and freshly ground pepper

SERVES 4–6 | **PREPARATION TIME** 25 minutes, plus overnight marinating |
COOKING TIME 20 minutes

JERK PORK WITH MANGO SALSA

Jerk pork can be found all over Jamaica, from the smartest restaurants to roadside
stands. The jerk paste, with typical ingredients of allspice and Scotch Bonnet chillies,
was probably originally used to preserve meat, but now it is popular for its spicy kick.
If you want really hot jerk pork, then use three chillies instead of two.

1] Put the jerk paste ingredients into a blender or food processor. Blend everything to
   a paste, adding 1 tablespoon water, if necessary.
2] Using a small sharp knife, poke holes into the pork fillets to allow the marinade to
   penetrate slightly. Rub the jerk paste all over the pork, then wrap each fillet tightly in
   cling film and leave to marinate in the fridge for 8 hours or overnight.
3] Mix together all the salsa ingredients and season with salt and pepper, to taste. Put in
   the fridge until needed.
4] Preheat the grill to high. Unwrap the pork and grill for 18–20 minutes, turning regularly,
   until the pork is a little charred on the outside but still slightly pink in the middle. Cover
   the pork with foil and leave to rest for 10 minutes before slicing. Serve the pork with the
   mango salsa and baked sweet potatoes.

1 tbsp vegetable oil
2 shallots, finely chopped
1 garlic clove, crushed
1 fresh red chilli, deseeded and finely chopped
a pinch of dried chilli flakes
2.5cm/1in piece fresh ginger, peeled and grated
5 tbsp apricot jam
150ml/5fl oz/scant ⅔ cup tomato ketchup
1½ tbsp Worcestershire sauce
1½ tbsp cider vinegar
2 tsp Dijon mustard

4 pork chops on the bone, each about
  200g/7oz, fat trimmed
1 handful of coriander leaves
salt and freshly ground black pepper
baby leaf spinach salad, to serve

YELLOW RICE
200g/7oz/1 cup basmati rice
1 tsp turmeric
1 cinnamon stick, about 10cm/4in
15g/½oz unsalted butter

SERVES 4 | **PREPARATION TIME** 30 minutes, plus overnight marinating |
COOKING TIME 35 minutes

SOUTH AFRICAN PORK CHOPS WITH YELLOW RICE

1] Put the oil in a medium-sized saucepan over a medium heat. Fry the shallots, garlic and fresh and dried chillies for 5–6 minutes, stirring, until the shallots are softened but not coloured. Add the ginger and cook for 1 minute. Remove from the heat and stir in the jam, ketchup, Worcestershire sauce, vinegar and mustard. Leave to cool completely.

2] Put the pork chops in a non-metallic dish and season with salt and pepper. Add the marinade and turn the chops until evenly coated. Cover and leave to marinate in the fridge for 8 hours or overnight.

3] Preheat the oven to 180°C/350°F/Gas 4. Line a baking sheet with baking paper. Remove the chops from the marinade, shaking off any excess, and put them on the baking sheet. Reserve the marinade. Roast the chops for 15–20 minutes until just cooked.

4] Meanwhile, make the yellow rice. Rinse the rice under cold running water until it runs clear. Transfer the rice to a medium-sized saucepan and add the turmeric, cinnamon stick and ½ teaspoon salt. Pour in 500ml/17fl oz/2 cups water and bring to the boil over a medium heat, stirring occasionally. Turn the heat down to low, cover and cook the rice for 10 minutes until the water is absorbed. Remove from the heat and leave to stand for 10 minutes, then remove the cinnamon stick and stir in the butter with a fork, fluffing the rice up as you stir.

5] Transfer the reserved marinade to a small saucepan and add 2 tablespoons water. Bring to the boil over a medium heat, then turn the heat down and simmer for 4–5 minutes until thickened. (Do not serve the marinade without boiling it first.)

6] Serve the rice topped with a chop and a spoonful of the warm marinade. Scatter the coriander over the top and serve with a baby leaf spinach salad.

2 tbsp vegetable oil
1 bunch of spring onions, thinly sliced
1 green pepper, deseeded and finely diced
1 garlic clove, crushed
1/4 tsp ground cumin
1/4 tsp cayenne pepper
3 fresh green chillies, deseeded and very finely diced
500g/1lb 2oz pork mince

2 tomatoes, deseeded and diced
250ml/9fl oz/1 cup vegetable stock
salt and freshly ground black pepper
12 taco shells, soured cream, fresh green chillies, deseeded and diced, 1 large avocado, pitted, peeled and thinly sliced, coriander leaves, 100g/3½oz mild Cheddar cheese, grated, and limes, cut into wedges, to serve

SERVES 4 | **PREPARATION TIME** 20 minutes | **COOKING TIME** 1½ hours

GREEN PORK CHILLI TACOS

Green pork chilli is slightly lighter than its tomato-based alternative, but it makes a perfect filling for tacos, because it doesn't overpower the flavour of the accompaniments. You can also serve the chilli with warm corn tortillas instead of the tacos, if you like.

1] Put 1 tablespoon of the oil in a medium-sized cast iron casserole or heavy-based saucepan over a medium heat. Add the spring onions and green pepper and cook for 8–10 minutes until softened. Add the garlic, cumin, cayenne pepper and chillies and cook for 2 minutes, stirring. Transfer to a bowl and leave to one side.

2] Heat the remaining oil in the casserole and turn the heat up to high. Add the mince and cook, breaking it up with a wooden spoon, for about 10 minutes until any liquid has evaporated and the pork is browned. You may find it easier to cook the pork in two batches, because it can steam in its own juices if the pan is too crowded.

3] Return the pepper and onion mixture to the casserole and add the tomatoes and stock. Bring to the boil, stirring to dissolve any brown sediment around the edge of the pan. Turn the heat down to very low and simmer for about 1 hour, stirring occasionally, until the liquid has evaporated but the pork is still moist. Season with salt and pepper, to taste.

4] To serve, warm the tacos following the pack instructions. Sit the chilli in the middle of the table and let everyone help themselves by piling the chilli into the taco shells and topping them with the soured cream, green chillies, avocado, coriander and cheese. A squeeze of lime adds the finishing touch.

2 tbsp vegetable oil
1 onion, finely chopped
½ celery stalk, finely diced
½ carrot, finely diced
2 garlic cloves, crushed
2 tsp hot chilli powder
½ tsp ground cumin
500g/1lb 2oz pork mince
150ml/5fl oz/scant ⅔ cup red wine
  or chicken stock
½ tsp dried oregano

400g/14oz tinned chopped tomatoes
¼ tsp sugar
1 cinnamon stick, about 10cm/4in
1 bay leaf
400g/14oz tinned kidney beans, drained
20g/¾oz good-quality dark chocolate
  (70% cocoa solids)
salt and freshly ground black pepper
soured cream, coriander leaves, lime wedges
  and boiled jasmine or basmati rice, to serve

SERVES 4 | **PREPARATION TIME** 15 minutes | **COOKING TIME** 1 hour 30 minutes

MEXICAN CHILLI

A lovely chilli with the hint of chocolate, which takes the flavour to another level!

1] Put 1 tablespoon of the oil in a medium-sized cast iron casserole or heavy-based saucepan over a low heat. Add the onion, celery, carrot and garlic and cook gently, stirring, for about 10 minutes until translucent and softened. Add the chilli powder and cumin, turn the heat up to medium and cook, stirring occasionally, for 2 minutes. Transfer the vegetables to a bowl and leave to one side.

2] Heat the remaining oil in the pan and turn the heat up to high. Add the mince and cook, breaking it up with a wooden spoon, for about 10 minutes until any liquid has evaporated and the pork is browned. You may find it easier to cook the pork in two batches, because it can steam in its own juices if the pan is too crowded. Add the wine to the pan and bring to the boil, stirring with a spoon to dissolve the brown sediment around the edge of the pan, then bubble for about 5 minutes until reduced by half.

3] Return the vegetables to the pan with the oregano, tomatoes, sugar, cinnamon and bay leaf. Bring to the boil, then turn the heat down to low, cover the pan and simmer for 40 minutes. Uncover the pan, add the kidney beans and simmer for a further 20 minutes or until the sauce has thickened.

4] Remove the cinnamon stick and bay leaf. Stir in the chocolate until melted, then season with salt and pepper to taste. Top the chilli with spoonfuls of soured cream, coriander leaves and lime wedges. Serve with rice by the side.

SPICY & AROMATIC

2 tbsp vegetable oil
1 onion, finely chopped
1 garlic clove, crushed
1 tsp dried chilli flakes
3/4 tsp cayenne pepper
1/2 tsp mild chilli powder
1/2 tsp fresh oregano leaves
1 fresh red chilli, deseeded and diced
450g/1lb pork mince
4 sesame buns, split in half and toasted
4 large lettuce leaves
1 recipe quantity Chunky Chips (see page 215),
  to serve

TOMATO SALSA
4 tomatoes, skinned, deseeded and chopped
4 spring onions, thinly sliced
1 handful of coriander leaves, chopped
1 tbsp lime juice
salt and freshly ground black pepper

LIME CREAM
4 tbsp soured cream
finely grated zest of 1/2 lime
juice of 1 lime

SERVES 4 | **PREPARATION TIME** 20 minutes | **COOKING TIME** 20 minutes

HOT MEXICAN PORK BURGERS

You can choose how fiery you like these burgers, but remember that the salsa and lime cream will act as great heat "extinguishers".

1] To make the salsa, mix together all the ingredients in a non-metallic bowl. Season with salt and pepper to taste and leave to one side. Mix together the ingredients for the lime cream in a small bowl and leave to one side.

2] Put 1 tablespoon of the oil in a small frying pan over a medium heat. Add the onion and cook for 6–8 minutes until softened. Add the garlic, dried chilli, cayenne, chilli powder and oregano and cook for 2 minutes. Transfer to a small bowl and leave to cool slightly.

3] Add the fresh chilli and mince to the bowl and season with salt and pepper. Mix gently together and form into 4 burgers. Try not to squash the mixture too much or the burgers will become dense.

4] Put the remaining oil in a large frying pan over a medium heat. When the oil is shimmering, add the burgers and cook for 1 minute, then turn the heat down slightly and cook for a further 4 minutes until browned underneath. Flip the burgers and cook for another 3–4 minutes until just cooked through.

5] Serve the burgers in a sesame bun with lettuce and a spoonful each of the salsa and lime cream. Serve with chunky chips by the side.

750g/1lb 10oz pork shoulder, cut into
  2.5cm/1in cubes
½ tsp turmeric
½ tsp garam masala
¼ tsp cayenne pepper
¼ tsp salt
1 onion, roughly chopped
2 fresh green chillies, deseeded and roughly
  chopped

4 garlic cloves, peeled
2.5cm/1in piece fresh ginger, peeled
  and roughly chopped
1 tbsp vegetable oil
1 tbsp cumin seeds
¼ tsp mustard seeds
salt and freshly ground pepper
boiled basmati rice, to serve

SERVES 4 | **PREPARATION TIME** 15 minutes, plus marinating | **COOKING TIME** 2 hours 10 minutes

COORG PORK CURRY

Coorg, or *pandi,* **curry is a popular dish in the Kodagu region of southwest India. It is traditionally served with rice dumplings, but is also excellent with basmati rice.**

1] Put the pork in a bowl and sprinkle the turmeric, garam masala, cayenne pepper and salt over the top. Toss the pork to coat it in the spices, then leave to marinate, covered, for 30 minutes.

2] Put the onion, chillies, garlic and ginger into a food processor or blender and blitz to a paste, then leave to one side.

3] Put the oil in a medium-sized cast iron casserole or heavy-based saucepan over a high heat. When the oil is shimmering, add the pork and cook for 5–6 minutes, turning the pork regularly, until browned on the outside.

4] Add the onion paste and cook, stirring, for 5 minutes. Pour in 125ml/4fl oz/½ cup water. Bring to the boil, then turn the heat down to very low, cover with a lid and gently simmer for 1½ hours or until the pork is tender enough to cut easily with a table knife. Remove the lid and simmer the curry for 30 minutes, stirring occasionally, until the sauce has thickened.

5] Meanwhile, toast the cumin and mustard seeds in a dry frying pan for 3–4 minutes until the cumin starts to release its aroma and has turned slightly darker in colour.

6] Grind the spices to a powder in a mini food processor or using a pestle and mortar, then stir them into the curry at the end of the cooking time. Season with salt and pepper, to taste, and serve with basmati rice.

1 tsp cumin seeds

1 tsp coriander seeds

½ tsp mustard seeds

1 tsp dried chilli flakes

½ tsp black peppercorns

8 garlic cloves, crushed

5cm/2in piece fresh ginger, peeled and grated

2 tbsp red wine vinegar

1kg/2lb 4oz pork leg, cut into 2.5cm/1in cubes

2 tbsp vegetable oil

2 onions, thinly sliced

2 fresh red chillies, deseeded and diced

300ml/10½fl oz/scant 1¼ cups vegetable stock

2 tbsp tomato purée

salt

boiled basmati rice or naan breads and mango chutney (optional), to serve

SERVES 4–6 | **PREPARATION TIME** 20 minutes, plus overnight marinating | **COOKING TIME** 1 hour 20 minutes

PORK VINDALOO

Pork is the meat traditionally used in a Goan vindaloo curry. This is a particularly good version and is not overwhelmingly hot but aromatic and slightly tangy. If you can get dried Kashmiri chillies then use 6 of these, roughly chopped, instead of the chilli flakes.

1] Toast the cumin, coriander and mustard seeds with the chilli flakes and peppercorns in a dry frying pan for 3–4 minutes until they smell aromatic. Grind the spices in a mini food processor or using a pestle and mortar. Transfer to a large bowl and mix in the garlic, ginger and vinegar. Add the pork and toss to coat it in the spice paste. Cover and leave to marinate in the fridge for 8 hours or overnight.

2] Put the oil in a large cast iron casserole or heavy-based saucepan over a medium heat. Add the onions and cook for 8–10 minutes, stirring occasionally, until softened. Add the red chillies and cook for 1 minute, then add the pork and cook for a further 6–8 minutes, turning the pieces of pork regularly, until browned on the outside.

3] Stir in the stock and tomato purée and bring to the boil, then turn the heat down to very low, cover and gently simmer for 40 minutes, stirring occasionally. Uncover the pan and cook for a further 10–15 minutes until the sauce has thickened slightly.

4] Season with salt to taste and serve the curry with basmati rice. Mango chutney would also be a good accompaniment as its sweetness balances the slight sourness of the vinegar in the curry.

1 fresh mild green chilli, deseeded and
  chopped
5cm/2in piece fresh ginger, peeled and grated
8 cardamom pods, seeds removed and pods
  discarded
1/2 tsp ground cumin
1/2 tsp ground coriander
200ml/7fl oz Greek-style yogurt, plus extra
  to serve

750g/1lb 10oz pork leg, cut into 2.5cm/1in cubes
100g/3 1/2oz unsalted butter
2 onions, chopped
1 cinnamon stick, about 10cm/4in long
200ml/7fl oz/scant 1 cup double cream
1 handful of coriander leaves
salt and freshly ground black pepper
1 recipe quantity Buttered Rice (see page 217)
  or plain boiled basmati rice, to serve

SERVES 4 | PREPARATION TIME 20 minutes, plus overnight marinating | COOKING TIME 1 hour

PORK KORMA

The Greek-style yogurt adds an elegant finish to this popular mild curry.

1] Grind the chilli, ginger and cardamom seeds in a blender and blitz to a paste using a mini food processor or pestle and mortar. Transfer the paste to a large bowl and stir in the cumin, ground coriander and yogurt. Add the pork and toss to coat it in the marinade. Cover and leave to marinate in the fridge for 8 hours or overnight.

2] Preheat the oven to 180°C/350°F/Gas 4. Melt the butter in a medium-sized cast iron casserole or heavy-based saucepan over a medium heat. Add the onions and cook for 8–10 minutes, stirring occasionally, until softened. Add the pork and marinade and cook for another 5–7 minutes, turning occasionally, until the pork is browned on the outside.

3] Add 125ml/4fl oz/1/2 cup water and the cinnamon stick, cover, then transfer the pan to the oven and cook for 40 minutes. Check after 20 minutes, giving the curry a stir and adding an extra splash of water if it looks dry.

4] Remove the pan from the oven and stir in the cream. Re-cover with the lid and return to the oven for a further 20 minutes.

5] Season with salt and pepper to taste, then scatter the coriander leaves over. Serve topped with a spoonful of yogurt and with the buttered rice.

5 shallots, roughly chopped

2 garlic cloves, roughly chopped

2.5cm/1in piece fresh ginger, peeled and
  roughly chopped

2 fresh red bird's eye chillies

1 tbsp vegetable oil

1kg/2lb 4oz pork leg, cut into 2.5cm/1in cubes

250ml/9fl oz/1 cup tinned coconut milk

2 lemongrass stalks, tough outer leaves
  removed, bruised

5 cardamom pods

3 kaffir lime leaves

1 cinnamon stick, about 10cm/4in long

1 star anise

1 tbsp soy sauce

1 tbsp soft dark brown sugar

4 tbsp toasted flaked coconut (optional)

1 handful of coriander leaves

COCONUT RICE

200g/7oz/1 cup jasmine or basmati rice

150ml/5fl oz/scant 2/3 cup tinned coconut milk

salt

SERVES 4–6 | PREPARATION TIME 30 minutes | COOKING TIME 1 hour 50 minutes

INDONESIAN CURRIED PORK WITH COCONUT RICE

This recipe is based on *Rendang*, which is an aromatic, chilli-hot curry that originated in Indonesia, but is now popular all over Southeast Asia. It is not a typical curry since there is very little sauce, instead the meat is infused with the intense flavour of the spices. If you want a less spicy version, remove the seeds from the chillies before making the paste.

1] Put the shallots, garlic, ginger and chillies into a blender or food processor and blend to a paste.

2] Put the oil in a wok or large frying pan over a medium-high heat. (You will need a lid for the wok or pan.) When the oil is shimmering, add the paste and fry for 2 minutes. Add the pork and cook for 5–6 minutes, turning occasionally, until browned all over.

3] Add the coconut milk and aromatics to the wok and bring to the boil. Turn the heat down to low and cover, then simmer gently for 45 minutes. Uncover the wok, stir in the soy sauce and sugar, then simmer for a further 45–55 minutes until there is no liquid left in the wok and the pork is sizzling.

4] Meanwhile, put the rice in a sieve and rinse under cold running water until it runs clear. Leave to drain for 2 minutes, then transfer to a medium-sized saucepan and add the coconut milk and 230ml/7¾fl oz/scant 1 cup water. Bring to the boil, add a pinch of salt, then turn the heat down to its lowest setting, cover and simmer gently for 10 minutes until there is no liquid left in the pan and the rice is tender. Turn off the heat and leave to stand, still covered, for 10 minutes, then fluff up the rice with a fork.

5] Serve the pork with the coconut rice, scattered with the flaked coconut, if using, and the coriander.

1.25kg/2lb 12oz pork spare ribs, cut individually
1 tsp paprika
125ml/4fl oz/½ cup rice wine vinegar
125ml/4fl oz/½ cup soy sauce
375ml/13fl oz/1½ cups vegetable stock
1 bay leaf
12 black peppercorns

3 garlic cloves, peeled
1 tbsp cornflour
1 tbsp clear honey
2 tbsp vegetable oil
2 spring onions, thinly sliced
freshly ground black pepper
boiled jasmine or basmati rice, to serve

SERVES 4 | **PREPARATION TIME** 20 minutes, plus marinating | **COOKING TIME** 1¾ hours

FILIPINO SWEET & SOUR PORK

Filipino cooking takes its influences from many parts of the world. Considered the national dish of the Philippines, this dish, otherwise known as *adobo*, takes its name from the Spanish word "marinade", and is typically a balance of sweet, sour and salty flavours.

1] Put the ribs in a bowl and sprinkle with the paprika. Season with ground black pepper and pour the vinegar and soy sauce over. Turn to coat the ribs in the marinade and leave to marinate for 30 minutes.

2] Put a large cast iron casserole or heavy-based saucepan over a medium heat. Add the ribs, marinade and vegetable stock; it should come halfway up the ribs, but if there is not enough, top up with water. Add the bay leaf and peppercorns. Roughly crush the garlic cloves with the back of a knife and add to the pan.

3] Bring the liquid to the boil, then turn the heat down to very low, cover and simmer for 1–1½ hours until the pork is tender. Turn the ribs over every 30 minutes.

4] Remove the cooked ribs and pat dry with kitchen paper. Skim any fat from the surface of the sauce, then bring to the boil and boil until reduced by half. Mix the cornflour with 1 tablespoon water and whisk this into the sauce with the honey. Return the sauce to the boil and cook for 1–2 minutes until thickened slightly. Keep the sauce warm.

5] Put the oil in large frying pan over a medium-high heat. Add the ribs and cook until browned all over. Transfer to a large serving bowl and pour the sauce over. Sprinkle with the spring onion slices and serve with jasmine rice.

CHAPTER 4

SLOW-COOKED

Cooking slow and low is a technique that suits many dishes, from slow-roasting a pork belly in a low oven, or braising a ham hock in a little wine, to the gentle simmering of a hearty stew. Yet they all yield the same result – moist, tender, flavourful meat. Like most meats, the best cuts of pork for slow cooking are the tougher ones: the muscles that do the most work. They usually have a high proportion of marbled fat and connective tissue and these melt into the cooking liquid, resulting in an unctuous sauce. Try Pork Cheeks with Caramelized Fennel to see how a cut that looks quite unpromising can become a restaurant-worthy dish, or Sticky Barbecue Ribs for pork that is so tender it literally falls off the bone.

Slow-cooked pork also has the advantage of needing very little attention during cooking, while still producing some impressively good dishes. Who could resist Slow-roasted Pork Belly with its crispy crackling or an Eight-hour Roast Shoulder of Pork, which is so tender that it can be cut with a fork? Any festive table would also welcome a Home-cooked Ham in Ginger & Mustard Glaze.

Slow-cooked dishes also reheat well and are often better if cooled, stored in the fridge and then reheated when needed. Try Pork Goulash for an excellent family meal or Chinese Pork Belly with Seasoned Rice for something slightly smarter. Whatever dish you choose to make, you'll find slow cooking is a wonderful and satisfying way to prepare pork.

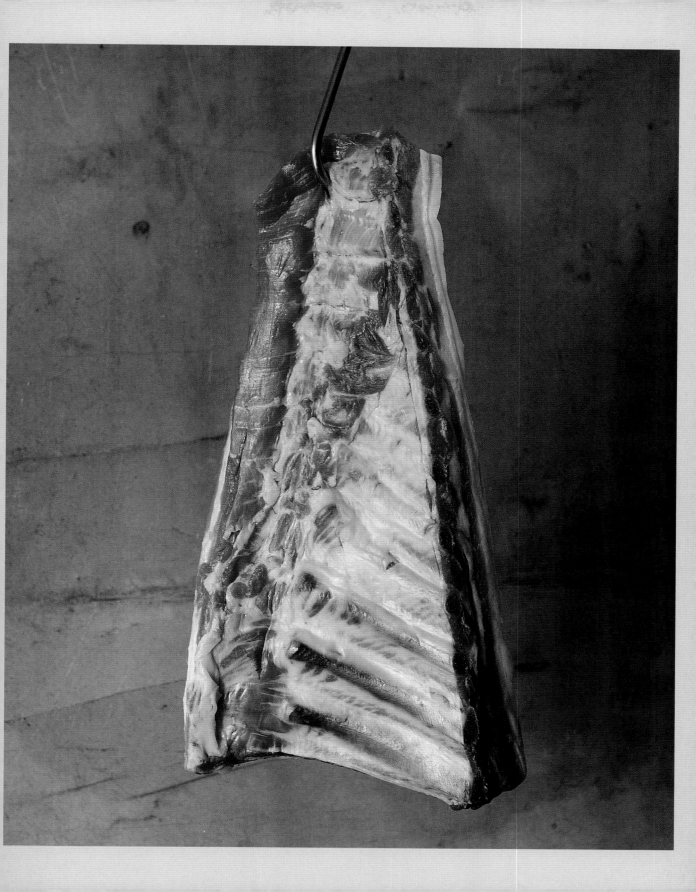

4 pigs' ears, trimmed
1 onion, quartered
1 carrot, scrubbed and halved
1 celery stalk, halved
6 black peppercorns
1 thyme sprig
1 bay leaf

85g/3oz/⅔ cup plain flour
vegetable oil, for deep frying
cayenne pepper, to season
salt
1 recipe quantity Apple Sauce (see page 213),
    or a green salad dressed in lemon and
    olive oil, to serve

SERVES 4 | **PREPARATION TIME** 30 minutes, plus cooling | **COOKING TIME** 2 hours

CRISPY PIGS' EARS

A very popular dish whenever it's on the menu. This often unused part of the pig has a fantastic texture when fried until crisp.

1] Wash the ears thoroughly and put them in a large saucepan. Cover with cold water and add the onion, carrot, celery, peppercorns, thyme and bay leaf. Bring to the boil over a high heat, then skim away any foamy scum that rises to the surface. Cover the pan, turn the heat down to low and simmer for 1½ hours until the ears are very soft. Drain the ears, discarding the solids, and leave them to cool to room temperature.

2] Put the ears on a large chopping board and cut them into 3mm/⅛in wide strips. Pat the strips as dry as possible with kitchen paper.

3] Pour enough oil in a deep saucepan or deep-fat fryer to fill by one-third. Heat the oil to 180°C/350°F. Line a baking sheet with a double layer of kitchen paper.

4] Put the flour into a bowl. Take a small handful of the ear strips and toss them in the flour, then carefully drop them, a couple at a time, into the hot oil. Take care because the ears are likely to spit as they go into the oil. Fry for 2 minutes or until crisp and golden brown. Using a slotted spoon, scoop the cooked strips out of the fat and transfer to the lined baking sheet to drain. Cook the remaining ear strips in batches, making sure that the oil is reheated between each batch.

5] Season the cooked strips with cayenne pepper and salt and serve with apple sauce. Alternatively, scatter the strips over a dressed green salad.

200g/7oz shredded cooked pork from the
  Eight-hour Roast Shoulder of Pork recipe
  (see page 170)
5 tbsp plum sauce
16 rice paper wrappers, about 22cm/8½in
  in diameter
1 large handful of mint leaves
1 large handful of basil leaves
1 large handful of coriander leaves
1 cucumber, deseeded and cut into matchsticks

2 large carrots, cut into matchsticks
1 bunch of spring onions, sliced into thin
  strips lengthways

DIPPING SAUCE
4 tbsp sugar
4 tbsp lime juice
4 tbsp fish sauce
2 fresh green bird's eye chillies, thinly sliced

SERVES 4 (makes 16) | **PREPARATION TIME** 40 minutes, plus the Eight-hour Roast Shoulder
of Pork and chilling

VIETNAMESE PORK SUMMER ROLLS

**This simple dish uses the leftovers from the Eight-hour Roast Shoulder of Pork, but you
could also use a similar slow-cooked pork that can be shredded with a fork. The rolls are
also good with sweet chilli sauce if you don't want to make the dip.**

1] Mix together the pork and plum sauce in a bowl. Set out a large bowl of warm water,
a chopping board or tray lined with kitchen paper and a second chopping board for
forming the rolls. Line a baking sheet with baking paper and leave to one side. It is
easiest to make the rolls one at a time.

2] Soak a rice paper wrapper in warm water for 1–2 minutes until softened. Transfer it to
the board lined with kitchen paper, blot away any excess water, then carefully lift the
wrapper onto the second board. Lay a couple of mint leaves in a line across the centre
of the wrapper, leaving a 2.5cm/1in border of rice wrapper on either side. Repeat with
a couple of basil leaves and 2–3 coriander leaves. Spoon a heaped tablespoon of the pork
on top of the herbs, then add a few pieces of cucumber, carrot and spring onion.

3] Fold the short sides of the wrapper over the filling, then carefully fold the bottom of
the wrapper over the filling and roll up tightly. Transfer the roll to the prepared lined
baking sheet. Repeat with the remaining wrappers and filling. Once all the rolls have
been made, cover with very lightly dampened kitchen paper and put in the fridge for
up to 2 hours.

4] To make the dip, mix together all the ingredients with 4 tablespoons warm water until
the sugar has dissolved, then refrigerate until needed.

5] To serve, divide the dipping sauce into small bowls. Cut each roll in half on the diagonal
and serve with the sauce.

2 tbsp olive oil

1 onion, finely chopped

1 carrot, finely diced

1 celery stalk, finely diced

2 garlic cloves, crushed

500g/1lb 2oz pork shoulder, cut into 2.5cm/
  1in cubes

150ml/5fl oz/scant ⅔ cup red wine

400g/14oz tinned chopped tomatoes

150ml/5fl oz/scant ⅔ cup beef stock

4 thyme sprigs

6 juniper berries

400g/14oz dried pappardelle

salt and freshly ground black pepper

finely grated Parmesan cheese, to serve

SERVES 4 | **PREPARATION TIME** 15 minutes | **COOKING TIME** 3 hours 45 minutes

PORK IN RED WINE WITH PAPPARDELLE

This is my version of the popular Tuscan *pappardelle al cinghiale*, or pasta with wild boar. Pork shoulder is an excellent alternative to wild boar and like many slow-cooked dishes, the sauce is even better if chilled overnight and reheated the next day.

1] Put 1 tablespoon of the oil in a medium-sized cast iron casserole or heavy-based saucepan over a low heat. Add the onion, carrot, celery and garlic and cook for 8–10 minutes, stirring occasionally, until the vegetables have softened but not coloured. Transfer the vegetables to a plate and leave to one side.

2] Turn the heat up to medium-high. Add half of the remaining oil and brown the pork for 6–8 minutes in two batches. Add the rest of the oil before cooking the second batch of pork.

3] Return the vegetables and pork to the pan and pour in the wine. Bring to the boil and cook for 5–8 minutes or until the wine has reduced by half, stirring occasionally to remove any brown sediment on the bottom of the pan. Add the tomatoes, stock, thyme and juniper berries. Return to the boil, then turn the heat down to very low and simmer, covered, for 1½ hours, stirring occasionally.

4] Uncover the pan and continue to simmer very gently for 1½ hours until the pork is falling to pieces and the sauce has thickened. Stir occasionally, making sure that the sauce doesn't catch on the bottom of the pan. Remove from the heat and stir the sauce with a fork to tear the meat into small shreds. Remove the thyme stalks and juniper berries and season with salt and pepper to taste. Keep the sauce warm.

5] Cook the pappardelle in a pan of boiling salted water for about 12 minutes until al dente. Drain, reserving a cupful of the cooking water. Toss the pasta with the sauce, adding a little of the pasta cooking water if the sauce needs it. Serve with grated Parmesan.

1 tbsp soft light brown sugar
1 tsp paprika
1 tsp mild chilli powder
1 tsp salt
1 tsp freshly ground black pepper
½ tsp cayenne pepper
2.25kg/5lb spare ribs, preferably as a rack but
  can be cut individually
2 tbsp vegetable oil
corn on the cob, baked potatoes and butter,
  to serve

BARBECUE SAUCE
300ml/10½fl oz/scant 1¼ cups tomato
  ketchup
200ml/7fl oz/scant 1 cup cola
1 tbsp white wine vinegar
1 tbsp clear honey
2 tsp Dijon mustard
1 tsp Worcestershire sauce

SERVES 4 | PREPARATION TIME 30 minutes, plus overnight marinating |
COOKING TIME 3¼ hours

STICKY BARBECUE RIBS

This makes a great alternative to the traditional Sunday roast. Putting the ribs in the oven early on a Sunday morning fills the house with the aromas of a great meal to come. The sharp, yet sweet, barbecue sauce is a must.

1] Mix together the sugar, paprika, chilli powder, salt, pepper and cayenne pepper. Rub the spice mixture all over the ribs, then cover and put in the fridge for 8 hours, or overnight.

2] To make the barbecue sauce, put all the ingredients in a medium-sized saucepan over a medium heat. Bring to the boil, stirring frequently, then turn the heat down slightly and simmer for about 20 minutes until reduced by half. Leave to cool, then refrigerate until needed. (The sauce can be made up to 5 days in advance.) Divide the sauce in half, and set one half aside for serving.

3] Preheat the oven to 150°C/300°F/Gas 2. Put the oil in a large roasting tin over a medium-high heat. When the oil is shimmering, cook the ribs for 6–8 minutes, turning once, until browned all over.

4] Remove the ribs from the tin, brush them with some of the remaining sauce, then return them to the tin, bone-side down. Cover the tin tightly with foil and roast for 2 hours until the meat is very tender.

5] Turn the oven up to 220°C/425°F/Gas 7. Remove the foil and roast the ribs for a further 40 minutes, brushing them with a little extra sauce and turning the pan every 10 minutes. (If the ribs are cut individually, roast them for 30 minutes at this stage.)

6] Transfer the ribs to a platter, separating them if necessary. Serve the ribs with the reserved sauce, corn on the cob and baked potatoes topped with butter.

"SHOW ME HOW" TO MARINATE THE RIBS

2kg/4lb 8oz boneless pork shoulder, skin
   scored, rolled and tied with string
1–2 tsp vegetable oil
1 tsp fennel seeds
1 tsp coarse sea salt
2 celery stalks
1 large carrot, quartered lengthways
1 onion, quartered

1 lemon, thinly sliced
250ml/9fl oz/1 cup dry white wine
250ml/9fl oz/1 cup vegetable stock
2 tsp cornflour
freshly ground black pepper
1 recipe quantity Johnnie's Mashed Potatoes
   (see page 215) or Goose Fat Roast Potatoes
   (see page 216) and green vegetables, to serve

SERVES 4 (with leftovers) | **PREPARATION TIME** 20 minutes | **COOKING TIME** 8 hours 35 minutes

EIGHT-HOUR ROAST SHOULDER OF PORK

Slow-roasted pork is fantastically easy as it pretty much looks after itself. The slow cooking results in meat so tender it can be cut with a fork. It makes sense to cook a large joint so that there are leftovers to make the Vietnamese Pork Summer Rolls (see page 166), or mix with barbecue sauce (see page 168) and serve in a soft roll.

1] Preheat the oven to 220°C/425°F/Gas 7. Pat the skin of the pork dry with kitchen paper, then rub it all over with a little oil. Grind the fennel seeds and salt together using a mini food processor or pestle and mortar and add plenty of black pepper. Rub the mixture all over the pork, making sure it gets into the cuts in the skin.

2] Put the celery, carrot and onion in the bottom of a medium-sized roasting tin. Scatter the lemon slices over and sit the pork on top. Roast for 30 minutes or until the skin starts to blister and crackle. Turn the oven down to 130°C/250°F/Gas 1 and tip the wine into the roasting tin. Roast the pork for 8 hours, turning the tin around halfway through the cooking time. The pork is ready when it is so tender that you can pull pieces away with a fork and the crackling is crisp.

3] Transfer the pork to a warm plate to rest. Strain the juices in the roasting tin through a sieve into a saucepan, discarding the lemon slices. Press the vegetables through the sieve with the back of a wooden spoon to extract as much liquid as possible. Add the stock and put the pan over a low heat. Mix the cornflour with 2 teaspoons water, then whisk it into the pan. Bring to the boil, stirring, then turn the heat down and simmer for 1 minute until thickened. Strain the gravy into a warm gravy boat or jug.

4] Remove the string from the pork and cut off the crackling. Cut or tear the pork into chunks and break the crackling into pieces. Serve the pork with the gravy, mashed potatoes and green vegetables.

750g/1lb 10oz pork shoulder, cut into
   2.5cm/1in cubes
rice or tortillas, coriander leaves and lime
   wedges, to serve

SPICE PASTE
1½ tsp coriander seeds
½ tsp black peppercorns
½ tsp cumin seeds
3 whole cloves
½ tsp salt
½ tsp turmeric

½ tsp mild chilli powder
½ tsp dried oregano
5 garlic cloves, crushed
4 tbsp fresh orange juice
4 tbsp fresh lime juice

PINEAPPLE SALSA
¼ large ripe pineapple, skin removed,
   cored and finely diced
1 small red onion, very finely chopped
juice of 1 lime

SERVES 4 | **PREPARATION TIME** 20 minutes, plus overnight marinating | **COOKING TIME** 3 hours

MEXICAN PORK SHOULDER

The combination of aromatics gives a distinctive taste to this slow-cooked roasted pork, while the kick from the pineapple salsa is guaranteed to set your taste buds tingling!

1] To make the spice paste, toast the coriander seeds, peppercorns, cumin seeds and cloves in a dry frying pan over a medium heat until they smell aromatic. Grind using a mini food processor or pestle and mortar, then transfer to a non-metallic bowl and mix in the remaining paste ingredients. Add the pork and turn in the marinade until evenly coated. Cover the bowl tightly and marinate overnight in the fridge.

2] Preheat the oven to 170°C/325°F/Gas 3. Line a large roasting tin with foil, leaving a good overhang, then line the foil with a similar sized sheet of baking paper. Spread the pork out in the lined tin, fold the baking paper and foil over the pork, then scrunch the edges of the foil together to form a sealed parcel. Bake for 3 hours until the pork is very tender and it can be cut with a fork.

3] While the pork is cooking, mix together the ingredients for the pineapple salsa in a non-metallic bowl and leave to one side.

4] Put the pork on a serving platter and flake it into pieces with a fork. You can spoon it onto cooked rice or serve with tortillas, adding spoonfuls of salsa, a few coriander leaves and a squeeze of lime juice.

1kg/2lb 4oz boneless pork loin, skin and fat
  removed
4 tbsp fennel seeds
1.75kg/3lb 12oz/6¼ cups coarse sea salt
2 egg whites
1 fennel bulb, trimmed and sliced
boiled baby new potatoes, to serve

FENNEL & ORANGE SALAD
2 large fennel bulbs, trimmed and sliced
  crossways
2 oranges, peeled and segmented
finely grated zest of 1 orange
2 tbsp extra virgin olive oil
salt and freshly ground black pepper

SERVES 4–6 | PREPARATION TIME 20 minutes, plus resting | COOKING TIME 1½ hours

PORK LOIN IN A FENNEL SALT CRUST

Baking in a salt crust is a traditional Mediterranean method of cooking, and it is an excellent way of retaining moisture in pork, leaving it juicy, tender and perfectly seasoned. The pork is served with a fragrant fennel and orange salad, although spinach sautéed in a little butter would also be delicious.

1] Preheat the oven to 130°C/250°F/Gas 1. Make sure all the fat, connective tissue and silverskin has been removed from the pork, then season all over with pepper.

2] Roughly grind the fennel seeds using a mini food processor or pestle and mortar. Put the coarse sea salt in a mixing bowl. Whisk the egg whites until slightly frothy, then stir them into the salt with the fennel seeds until combined.

3] Put a 1cm/½in thick layer of the salt mixture in the bottom of a roasting tin. Lay the fennel slices on top, making a bed of fennel just slightly larger than the pork. Sit the pork on top, then pack the remaining salt over and around the pork, forming a thick crust. Roast in the oven for 1½ hours. If you want to check the pork after this time, then insert a thin metal skewer through the crust and into the centre of the meat – it is ready when the juices run clear.

4] Meanwhile, to make the salad, arrange the fennel and orange slices on a large platter. Sprinkle with the orange zest, season with a little salt and pepper and drizzle with the olive oil. Leave to one side until ready to serve.

5] Remove the tin from the oven and leave the pork to rest for 30 minutes. Use a knife to break through the crust, then transfer the pork to a board and brush away any residual salt. Cut the pork into thin slices. Serve with baby new potatoes and the fennel and orange salad.

"SHOW ME HOW" TO MAKE THE SALT CRUST

6 fresh beetroots
1kg/2lb 4oz boneless pork loin
3 garlic cloves, sliced
2 tbsp vegetable oil
4–5 large handfuls of unsprayed hay

125ml/4fl oz/½ cup crème fraîche
2 tbsp freshly grated horseradish
a squeeze of lemon juice
salt and freshly ground black pepper
boiled new potatoes, to serve

SERVES 4–6 | **PREPARATION TIME** 20 minutes | **COOKING TIME** 2 hours

HAY-BAKED PORK LOIN

Baking in hay is a very old cooking technique. The hay provides moisture and also acts as insulation, letting the meat cook gently in the residual heat of the oven. You can buy unsprayed hay, which is free from pesticides, from a pet store.

1] Put the beetroots in a saucepan and cover with cold water. Bring up to the boil over a high heat, then turn the heat down slightly and blanch for 25 minutes until part-cooked, then drain.

2] Meanwhile, preheat the oven to 130°C/250°F/Gas 1. Using a sharp knife, remove the skin and most of the fat from the pork. If you want the pork to keep a nice round shape, tie it with 3–4 pieces of string. Using a sharp knife, make slits in the pork and insert a slice of garlic into each one, pushing it into the meat. Season the pork with salt and pepper. Put the oil in a large frying pan over a high heat. When the oil is shimmering, add the pork and brown it all over, including the ends.

3] Put a handful of the hay in the bottom of a large cast iron casserole or a heavy-based ovenproof saucepan. Sit the pork on the hay and surround it with the part-cooked beetroots. Pack more hay around and over the top of the pork and beetroots. Cover with the lid.

4] Put the casserole in the oven and cook for 45 minutes, then turn the oven off, leaving the door slightly ajar, and let the pork and beetroot sit in the oven for a further 45 minutes. Remove the beetroots and peel away the skins and slice thinly.

5] Mix together the crème fraîche and horseradish, then season with salt and a squeeze of lemon juice.

6] Remove the pork from the hay. Slice it thinly and serve with the beetroots and a spoonful of the horseradish crème fraîche. A serving of new potatoes would be perfect.

"SHOW ME HOW" TO STUD THE LOIN AND BAKE IN HAY

1.25kg/2lb 12oz boneless pork loin, skin
  and fat removed
1.8kg/4lb boneless pork belly
3 rosemary sprigs
leaves from 8 thyme sprigs
10 garlic cloves, peeled
finely grated zest of 1 lemon

1½ tsp coarse sea salt, plus extra for sprinkling
12 sage leaves
1–2 tsp vegetable oil
freshly ground black pepper
1 recipe quantity Goose Fat Roast Potatoes
  (see page 216), Apple Sauce (see page 213)
  and green vegetables, to serve

SERVES 8–10 | **PREPARATION TIME** 40 minutes, plus standing and resting |
COOKING TIME 2¼ hours

PORCHETTA WITH HERBS & GARLIC

Porchetta was originally a boned, stuffed and rolled whole pig, most commonly cooked
for feasts and festivals. Using pork loin wrapped in a piece of pork belly captures the
best parts of this traditional dish; the fattier belly yields plenty of crisp skin and protects
the leaner loin, keeping it deliciously moist. You will need to buy pieces of meat that are
relatively the same size and it is a good idea to ask your butcher to help with this, but it
is well worth the effort for this truly celebratory roast. And apple sauce is a must!

1] Using a sharp knife, trim away any excess meat from the side of the loin to leave a nice
round piece of meat, often referred to as the eye. (The trimmed part of the pork loin can
be sliced thinly and used in a stir fry.) Score the skin of the belly at 5mm/¼in intervals
(or ask your butcher to do this for you), taking care not to cut into the flesh. Turn the
belly over and make long cuts down the length of the flesh, then make several long cuts
along the width.

2] Finely chop the needles from two of the rosemary sprigs, then grind with the thyme,
garlic, lemon zest and sea salt using a mini food processor or pestle and mortar to make
a coarse paste. Season with plenty of pepper. Rub the herb paste into the flesh side of
the pork belly, making sure it gets into the cuts and is evenly coated, and arrange the
sage leaves on top of the paste-coated flesh.

3] Sit the loin on top of the herb-coated belly and bring the edges of the belly together to
wrap around the loin. Tie the joint at 5cm/2in intervals with string, then sit it on a wire
rack that is set over a roasting tin. Pat the skin dry with kitchen paper and leave to stand
at room temperature for 2 hours.

4] Preheat the oven to 220°C/425°F/Gas 7.

5] Just before roasting, rub the skin of the porchetta with a little vegetable oil, then using a sharp paring knife, make small holes in the skin. Insert the needles from the remaining rosemary sprig into the holes and season with extra salt and a little pepper.

6] Put the porchetta back on the wire rack set over a roasting tin. Roast for 45 minutes, turning halfway, until the skin begins to blister and crackle. Turn the oven down to 150°C/300°F/Gas 2 and roast for a further 1½ hours. (If your porchetta is significantly bigger, then allow 40 minutes per kg/18 minutes per lb of the total weight.) Remove from the oven and check that it is ready by inserting a metal skewer into the centre – the juices should run clear. If the juices are red, return it to the oven for a further 5 minutes and test again. Leave to rest for 30 minutes.

7] Traditionally, porchetta is cut into 1cm/½in thick slices (with crackling attached), but if you like thinner slices, remove the crackling before carving the meat.

8] Serve the porchetta with goose fat roast potatoes, apple sauce and green vegetables. Leftover cold porchetta makes the most fantastic filling for a sandwich.

JOHNNIE'S TIP

The porchetta can be assembled the day before serving and stored in the fridge. Make sure you remove it from the fridge 2 hours before roasting. Leave to stand, uncovered, at room temperature. Pat dry the skin with kitchen paper after 1 hour to remove any condensation that may have collected on the skin.

800g/1lb 12oz boneless pork loin,
   skin and most of the fat removed
15g/½ oz unsalted butter
1 tsp vegetable oil
500ml/17fl oz/2 cups whole milk
3 long strips of lemon rind pared
   from ½ lemon

1 garlic clove, peeled but left whole
1 bay leaf
1 thyme sprig
salt and freshly ground black pepper
1 recipe quantity Goose Fat Roast Potatoes
   (see page 216) and Green Beans with Garlic
   & Almonds (see page 218), to serve

SERVES 4 | **PREPARATION TIME** 15 minutes, plus resting | **COOKING TIME** 1¾ hours

SLOW-COOKED PORK IN MILK

Cooking the pork in milk keeps it moist and helps to tenderize the meat. The milk also cooks down into a thick sauce that is intensely flavoured with lemon, garlic and thyme. I have used a boneless pork loin for ease, but you could also use one on the bone if you have a large enough casserole.

1] Season the pork all over with salt and pepper. If you want the pork to keep a nice round shape, tie it with 3–4 pieces of string.

2] Put the butter and oil into a cast iron casserole or heavy-based saucepan that is large enough to fit the pork snugly and place over a medium heat. When foaming, add the pork and brown all over, not forgetting the ends.

3] Pour the milk into the pan; it should come halfway up the sides of the pork, so you may need slightly more or slightly less, depending on the size of your pan. Add the strips of lemon rind, the garlic, bay leaf and thyme. Bring to the boil, then turn the heat down to very low, partially cover and simmer for 1 hour, turning the pork over every 20 minutes. The milk may curdle, but this is normal.

4] Uncover the pan and cook the pork for a further 30 minutes until the sauce has reduced right down and has turned a light caramel colour. Stir the sauce regularly during this stage as it can burn very quickly. Check the seasoning, adding extra salt and pepper to taste.

5] Remove the pork from the sauce and leave to rest, covered, for 20 minutes, then remove the string, cut the meat into thin slices and set out on a platter. Gently reheat the sauce and spoon it over the pork. Serve with goose fat roast potatoes and green beans with garlic and almonds. The pork is also exceptionally good served cold.

200g/7oz/heaped 1½ cups OO pasta flour,
  plus extra for dusting
3 eggs
½ recipe quantity Confit of Pork Belly
  (see page 181)
10 cornichons, finely chopped
2 large handfuls of flat-leaf parsley leaves,
  chopped
finely grated zest of 1 lemon
salt and freshly ground black pepper
pea shoots or chopped parsley leaves,
  to serve

MADEIRA SAUCE
60g/2¼oz cold unsalted butter, cubed
1 shallot, very finely chopped
4 tbsp Madeira
250ml/9fl oz/1 cup beef stock
½–1 tsp lemon juice, to taste

SERVES 4 | **PREPARATION TIME** 1¾ hours, plus Confit of Pork Belly, resting and chilling | **COOKING TIME** 35 minutes

RAVIOLI OF CONFIT PORK

A spectacular dish to be served only to your nearest and dearest! You will need a pasta machine to make the ravioli.

1] To make the pasta, put the flour in a pile on a large work surface. Make a well in the centre and add one whole egg to the flour, then separate the remaining 2 eggs and add the yolks only. Using your fingertips, gradually incorporate the flour into the eggs to make a dough. If the dough is very dry or too stiff, then add a little of the leftover egg white, 1 teaspoon at a time, until it is slightly pliable. Knead for about 5 minutes until the dough is smooth and silky. You can also make the dough in a food processor, adding all of the ingredients and processing until you get a smooth ball of dough. Wrap the dough in cling film and leave it to rest at room temperature for 30 minutes.

2] Meanwhile, remove the skin from the confit pork and scrape away most of the fat. Shred then finely chop the meat and a little of the fat. Transfer to a bowl and mix in the cornichons, parsley and lemon zest. Season with a little salt and plenty of pepper.

3] Unwrap the pasta dough and divide into four equal pieces. Take one piece and re-wrap the remaining pieces until needed. Lightly dust a work surface with flour and set up the pasta rolling machine. Line a large baking sheet with cling film and generously dust it with flour. Feed the piece of dough through the widest setting of the pasta machine and repeat one or two times. Reduce the width of the rollers by one notch, then feed the pasta through the rollers. Repeat, working down through the width settings, until you have a long sheet of pasta. (If it becomes too long to work with, cut it in half widthways when you get to notch 5 on the machine and then the roll the two pieces separately.)

4] Using an 11cm/4¼in round cutter, cut out 6 circles of pasta. Lay out 3 circles and brush the edges with water. Put a heaped teaspoonful of the filling into the centre and lay a second circle of pasta on top. Carefully press the top of the pasta around the filling to expel the air and seal the dough. Pinch the edges together with your fingers, then use the cutter to neaten, if you like. Transfer the ravioli to the prepared baking sheet and cover with cling film. Repeat with the remaining pasta and filling, using a quarter of the pasta each time to prevent it drying out. The ravioli can be chilled for up to 3 hours before cooking.

5] To make the sauce, melt 10g/¼oz of the butter in a saucepan over a medium heat. When foaming, add the shallot and cook for 6–8 minutes until softened. Add the Madeira, increase the heat and boil until reduced by half, then add the stock and boil for 6–8 minutes until reduced by about half again. Turn the heat down to very low, then gradually whisk in the remaining butter until you have a smooth, glossy sauce. Season with salt and pepper and stir in the lemon juice, to taste. Put the sauce in a warm place and whisk it regularly while you cook the pasta.

6] Bring a large saucepan of salted water to the boil. Carefully drop the ravioli into the water and return to the boil. Turn the heat down and simmer for 5 minutes, turning the ravioli halfway so they cook evenly. Don't let the water boil rapidly. You will need to cook them in two or three batches, depending on the size of your pan.

7] Gently reheat the sauce. Using a perforated spoon, lift the ravioli from the water and pat the base of the spoon dry with kitchen paper as you lift each one out. Serve the ravioli with the sauce spooned over and sprinkled with the pea shoots or parsley.

1kg/2lb 4oz boneless pork belly, skin scored

5cm/2in piece fresh ginger, cut into 1cm/¼in thick slices

4 spring onions, trimmed

2 star anise

6 black peppercorns

3 tbsp Chinese cooking wine or dry sherry

1 tbsp soy sauce, plus extra to taste

1 tsp clear honey

1 recipe quantity Ginger Pak Choi (see page 217), to serve

SEASONED RICE

200g/7oz/1 cup jasmine or basmati rice

3 tbsp rice wine vinegar

2 tbsp mirin

2 tbsp caster sugar

a large pinch of salt

SERVES 4 | **PREPARATION TIME** 20 minutes, plus cooling and overnight chilling | **COOKING TIME** 7 hours over 2 days

CHINESE PORK BELLY WITH SEASONED RICE

This is a great dish for a dinner party because the pork can be braised a day or two ahead and finished just before serving. The pork belly can also be cut into smaller-sized pieces to serve as a starter.

1] Preheat the oven to 150°C/300°F/Gas 2.

2] Put the pork belly in a large casserole and add the ginger, spring onions, star anise, peppercorns, cooking wine and soy sauce. Add enough water to just cover the pork (about 2 litres/70fl oz/8 cups). If you don't have a large enough casserole, then use a roasting tin and cover it with a double layer of foil before transferring the pork to the oven.

3] Put the pan over a high heat and bring the liquid to the boil, then cover tightly with a lid and transfer to the oven. Cook for 6 hours or until the pork is very tender. Check the pork after 4 hours to see if the liquid needs topping up and add extra water, if needed. (Some will evaporate during cooking, but it should still come halfway up the sides of the pork.)

4] Remove the casserole from the oven, uncover and leave to cool for 30 minutes. Using a spatula, transfer the pork to a plate or baking sheet, but be careful as it is very tender and can break up. Leave to cool for a further 30 minutes, then cover with a large plate or another baking sheet, weight the top with a couple of filled cans and transfer to the fridge to chill overnight. Strain the cooking liquid into a container, leave to cool completely and then put it in the fridge overnight, too. [continued on page 188]

5] To finish the dish the next day, preheat the oven to 180°C/350°F/Gas 4. Line a baking sheet with a piece of baking paper. Put the pork belly onto a chopping board and, using a sharp knife, cut into four equal pieces. Put the pork, skin-side down, in a large non-stick frying pan. Put the pan over a low heat for 8 minutes or until the fat starts to melt out of the pork. Increase the heat to medium-high and cook for 4–5 minutes until the skin has darkened slightly and turned crisp (take care as it may spit a little at this point).

6] Transfer the pork to the prepared baking sheet, skin-side up, and put it in the oven (reserving the fat from the pork in the frying pan for future use). Cook for 20 minutes until the pork has heated through. Once the pork is hot, you can switch off the oven and leave the door slightly ajar and it will be fine sitting in the warm oven for a further 20 minutes if you are not ready to serve it straightaway.

7] In the meantime, make the seasoned rice. Put the rice in a saucepan and cover with water. Season with salt. Put the pan over a medium-high heat and bring to the boil. Turn the heat down to low, cover and simmer for 8–10 minutes until the rice is tender. Drain the rice and return it to the saucepan. Stir in the vinegar, mirin, sugar and salt and leave the pan to one side for a couple of minutes.

8] Skim and discard the fat that has settled on top of the cooking liquid, which should by now have set into a jelly. Transfer the jelly to a saucepan and bring to the boil over a high heat. Boil for 6–10 minutes until the liquid has reduced by half to about 150ml/ 5fl oz/scant ⅔ cup). Keep the sauce warm.

9] Serve the pork on top of the rice and the ginger pak choi with the sauce spooned over.

JOHNNIE'S TIP

To finish the pork in Step 6, for a really smart appearance when cutting the meat into portions, make sure the belly is fully chilled. Using a large, heavy, sharp knife, trim the sides of the belly to give it neat edges, then cut into four equal-sized portions ready for reheating. Any trimmings can be cut into dice and fried briefly as part of a stir-fry or oriental salad.

1 tbsp vegetable oil

1.5–2kg/3lb 5oz–4lb 8oz pork belly on the bone, skin unscored

3 tbsp coarse sea salt

2 onions, quartered

2 celery stalks, trimmed

3 carrots, halved lengthways

1 recipe quantity Sticky Red Cabbage (see page 219), Apple Jam (see page 213) and Johnnie's Mashed Potatoes (see page 215), to serve

SERVES 4 | **PREPARATION TIME** 30 minutes, plus resting | **COOKING TIME** 12 hours

SLOW-ROASTED PORK BELLY *[pictured overleaf]*

This cracking dish was the catalyst for writing this book, and I have to say it's the most popular meal I have ever had the pleasure to serve. Meat always tastes better if it is roasted on the bone, and although unusually the skin isn't scored in this recipe, I find it gives the best results.

1] Preheat the oven to 220°C/425°F/Gas 7.

2] Massage the oil all over the pork and sprinkle the salt over the skin. It may look like a lot of salt, but it helps to draw the moisture out of the skin, giving fantastic crackling. Sit the pork, skin-side up, on a bed of onions, celery and carrots in a roasting tin.

3] Roast the pork belly for 45 minutes until the skin starts to bubble and crackle at the edges. Turn the roasting tin, then reduce the temperature to 200°C/400°F/Gas 6. Roast for another 45 minutes, by which time there should be a bubbly glaze appearing on the skin. Now reduce the oven to 180°C/350°F/Gas 4, turn the tin again and cook for a further 45 minutes; then 150°C/300°F/Gas 2 for 45 minutes; then 130°C/250°F/Gas 1 for 45 minutes. Turn the roasting tin every time you reduce the oven temperature so that the pork cooks evenly in the oven.

4] Finally, roast the pork at 100°C/200°F/Gas ½ for 8 hours, turning the pan once more halfway. Remove from the oven, scrape off the excess salt and transfer the pork to a warm plate and rest for 20 minutes. Twist and pull out the bones and use a sharp knife to ease away the white cartilage attached to the meat. Cut into portions and serve the pork with sticky red cabbage, apple jam and mashed potatoes.

JOHNNIE'S TIP

If using a boneless pork belly, you will need a 1kg/2lb 4oz joint. Sit the pork belly on a roasting rack or on a bed of carrots, onions and celery. Reduce the cooking time at 100°C/200°F/Gas ½ to 3 hours.

"SHOW ME HOW" TO PREPARE AND BONE THE PORK BELLY

4 tbsp plain flour

750g/1lb 10oz pork leg, cut into 2.5cm/1in cubes

15g/½oz unsalted butter

1 large onion, thinly sliced

1 garlic clove, crushed

1–2 tbsp vegetable oil

1 tbsp paprika

½ tsp cayenne pepper

125ml/4fl oz/½ cup dry white wine

400g/14oz tinned chopped tomatoes

250ml/9fl oz/1 cup vegetable stock

1 bay leaf

1 red pepper, deseeded and cut in half lengthways

4 tbsp soured cream

1 handful of flat-leaf parsley leaves, chopped

salt and freshly ground black pepper

basmati rice or 1 recipe quantity Buttered Rice (see page 217), to serve

SERVES 4 | **PREPARATION TIME** 15 minutes | **COOKING TIME** 2½ hours

PORK GOULASH

This is a great variation on the usual beef recipe. For me, the pork adds more flavour to the sweet, slightly tangy creamy sauce.

1] Season the flour with plenty of salt and pepper in a large bowl. Toss the pork in the seasoned flour and transfer it to a plate, discarding any excess flour in the bowl.

2] Melt the butter in a large cast iron casserole or heavy-based saucepan over a medium heat. When foaming, add the onion and garlic and cook for 8–10 minutes until softened. Transfer the onion to a plate and turn the heat up to medium-high.

3] Add 1 tablespoon of the oil and, when shimmering, add half the pork and brown on all sides. Using a slotted spoon, remove the pork to a plate and then brown the remaining pork.

4] Return the first batch of pork and the onion mixture to the pan with the paprika and cayenne. Cook for 2 minutes, stirring, then add the wine and bring to the boil. Boil until the wine has reduced by half, then add the tomatoes, stock and bay leaf. Return to the boil, then turn the heat down to low, part-cover, and simmer for 2 hours or until the pork is tender enough to be cut with a fork.

5] Meanwhile, preheat the grill to high. Grill the red pepper, skin-side up, for 3–4 minutes until charred in places. Put the pepper in a bowl and cover tightly with cling film. Leave to cool. Peel away the skin, then cut the pepper into thin strips. Add to the goulash about 30 minutes before the end of the cooking time.

6] Season with salt and pepper to taste, then remove the goulash from the heat. Serve the goulash topped with the soured cream and parsley, and with rice by the side.

500g/1lb 2oz jarred or tinned sauerkraut, drained
30g/1oz unsalted butter
1 onion, thinly sliced
2 garlic cloves, thinly sliced
500ml/17fl oz/2 cups dry white wine, preferably a dry Riesling
1 bay leaf
4 juniper berries
2 thyme sprigs

4 black peppercorns
2 smoked ham steaks, each about 200g/7oz
2 tbsp vegetable oil
4 good-quality sausages
4 fresh or smoked pork chops, each about 200g/7oz
450g/1lb small white potatoes, peeled
1 large handful of flat-leaf parsley leaves, chopped

SERVES 4 (generously) | **PREPARATION TIME** 15 minutes | **COOKING TIME** 2½ hours

CHOUCROUTE

Choucroute can only be described as a pork feast with cabbage – it's certainly a hearty dish! It can be made with any combination of fresh, smoked and salted pork, so I have used widely available cuts, but feel free to make your own meaty substitutions.

1] Preheat the oven to 170°C/325°F/Gas 3. Rinse the sauerkraut under cold running water, then leave to drain in a colander.

2] Put the butter in a large cast iron casserole or heavy-based ovenproof saucepan over a low heat. When melted, add the onion and garlic and cook for 8–10 minutes, stirring occasionally, until softened. Add the sauerkraut, wine, bay leaf, juniper berries, thyme and peppercorns, then turn the heat up slightly and bring to the boil.

3] Nestle the ham steaks in the sauerkraut mixture, cover, then transfer to the oven and cook for 1½ hours. Towards the end of the cooking time, heat the oil in a large frying pan, add the sausages and chops and cook until browned, turning them occasionally. Don't overcrowd the frying pan – you will probably have to cook them in two batches.

4] Remove the casserole from the oven and check that there is still a little liquid left in the pan. If it is very dry, then add a splash of water or extra wine. Sit the sausages and chops on top of the sauerkraut, put the lid back on and bake for a final 30 minutes.

5] Meanwhile, put the potatoes in a large saucepan of salted water over a high heat. Bring to the boil, then turn the heat down and simmer for 20 minutes or until tender.

6] Cut each ham steak in two to give four portions. Pick out the bay leaf, juniper berries, thyme and peppercorns from the sauerkraut. Serve the choucroute with the potatoes. Scatter the parsley over the top before serving.

250g/9oz/1¼ cups dried haricot beans
1 tbsp duck or goose fat or vegetable oil
4 duck legs
4 Toulouse sausages
100g/3½oz lardons, cubetti di pancetta or diced thick smoked bacon
1 onion, finely chopped
1 carrot, diced
1 celery stalk, diced
4 garlic cloves, peeled
125ml/4fl oz/½ cup dry white wine
400g/14oz tinned chopped tomatoes
2 thyme sprigs
1 bay leaf
salt and freshly ground black pepper
crisp green salad, to serve

SERVES 4 | **PREPARATION TIME** 30 minutes, plus overnight soaking | **COOKING TIME** 3¼ hours

CASSOULET

A beautiful marriage of flavours, textures and different types of meat. This is a truly wonderful dish that deserves its place at any great dinner table.

1] Put the haricot beans in a large bowl and cover with plenty of cold water. Leave to soak overnight. Drain the beans, transfer them to a large saucepan and cover with plenty of fresh water. Put the saucepan over a high heat. Bring to the boil and then boil the beans briskly for 10 minutes. Drain the beans and set aside.

2] Put the duck fat in a large cast iron casserole or heavy-based ovenproof saucepan over a medium heat. When melted, add the duck legs, skin-side down, and brown for 5–6 minutes until the skin turns golden. Turn the duck legs and brown the flesh side, then transfer to a plate. Add the sausages and brown all over, then transfer to the plate.

3] Add the lardons, onion, carrot and celery to the casserole and cook for 6–8 minutes until the vegetables have softened. Add the beans, garlic, wine, tomatoes, thyme and bay leaf. Season with black pepper but no salt at this stage, because it will toughen the beans. Fill the tomato tin with water and add this too. Bring to the boil over a high heat, then turn the heat down, cover and simmer for 30 minutes. Preheat the oven to 170°C/325°F/Gas 3.

4] Nestle the duck legs and sausages into the beans. Return the lid and bake the cassoulet for 2 hours or until the beans are tender. Check the pan after 1 hour, and add a little extra water if it looks dry.

5] Just before serving, remove the duck legs and sausages from the pan. Pull the duck meat away from the bones in large chunks and slice the sausages thickly. Season the beans with salt and pepper, remove the bay leaf and thyme and mash the whole garlic cloves into the sauce. Serve the beans topped with the duck and sausages, and with a crisp green salad by the side.

HOW TO BRAISE PORK

Braise comes from the French word *braiser* – a tightly covered pot that sits on top of hot coals – though it has now become a universal culinary term for cooking meat and vegetables slowly in a covered container with a small amount of liquid.

The combination of low temperature, moist heat and long cooking time makes braising ideal for tougher cuts of meat and particularly ones that lack a good marbling of fat, such as pork leg or cheek. Having said that, fattier cuts like pork shoulder also braise well. You can also braise more tender cuts, such as tenderloin fillet or loin, but as these are usually cooked for only a short period of time, they can be more difficult to time correctly.

During the cooking process the meat transforms itself from tough and chewy to soft and tender. The joint of meat (you can also braise smaller pieces) is automatically basted while it cooks, because the steam from the cooking liquid hits the lid of the pot and then runs down onto the meat. As an added bonus, the connective tissues melt as gelatine into the cooking liquid, leaving an enriched sauce that can be served with the meat.

The casserole or pan should be fairly thick and heavy so that the heat during cooking is kept constant, and the lid needs to fit tightly to prevent any of the liquid evaporating. Braising can be done on the hob over a very low heat, or in the oven at a low temperature; either way there are five steps to follow. The first is to brown the meat. This has two purposes, firstly to add colour to the meat and secondly to create a *fond*, which comes from the browning of the meat and any caramelized juices that stick to the casserole, adding richness to the finished dish. Pat the meat dry and season it well with salt and pepper before browning, then add a little oil to the pan to help the process along. The meat should be browned over a medium heat – too low and the meat will just steam but too high and the bottom of the pan will start to burn, giving a bitter flavour to the finished dish.

The second stage is to add aromatics such as garlic, herbs and vegetables. Onions, carrots and celery are quite common, but other robust vegetables like fennel and parsnips can also be used. As the cooking time is long, the vegetables should be left in fairly large pieces.

The next step is to add liquid, and because not much is added it should be flavourful. Wine is a popular choice, although a good-quality stock is also great. Add the liquid to the pan and let it bubble, stirring, to start to release the *fond* or caramelized bits on the bottom and side of the casserole. It is important to cover the casserole with a tight-fitting lid so the meat can cook slowly in the oven or on the hob until tender.

The next stage, after cooking, is to let the braised joint rest for a short time off the heat. This lets the fibres in the meat relax, making it easier to cut. The final stage is finishing the sauce. The sauce may need reducing by boiling or thickening with a flour and butter paste, or it may need extra liquid adding to it, depending on the recipe.

"SHOW ME HOW" TO BRAISE THE PORK

2kg/4lb 8oz pork shoulder on the bone or
    1.25kg/2lb 12oz boneless joint
1 tbsp olive oil
1 large onion, thickly sliced
2 garlic cloves, bruised
1 large carrot, thickly sliced
1 celery stalk, thickly sliced

2 rosemary sprigs
finely grated zest and juice of 1 large orange
250ml/9fl oz/1 cup vegetable stock
300ml/10½fl oz/scant 1¼ cups fruity red wine
10g/¼oz unsalted butter, softened
2 tsp plain flour
salt and freshly ground black pepper

SERVES 4 (with leftovers) | **PREPARATION TIME** 20 minutes | **COOKING TIME** 4½ hours

RED WINE & ORANGE BRAISED PORK SHOULDER [*pictured overleaf*]

1] Preheat the oven to 170°C/325°F/Gas 3. Season the pork with salt and pepper.

2] Put the oil in a large casserole or heavy-based roasting tin over a medium heat. Brown the pork shoulder for 2–3 minutes on each side until browned all over. Remove from the casserole and leave to one side. Add the onion, garlic, carrot and celery and cook for 2–3 minutes. Return the pork to the casserole and add the rosemary and orange zest and juice. Pour in the stock and wine.

3] Turn the heat off and cover tightly with a lid (or a double layer of foil, if using the roasting tin). Transfer the casserole to the oven and cook for 4 hours or until the pork is very tender and falling away from the bone.

4] Remove the pork from the casserole and transfer to a warm plate. Cover with foil and leave in a warm place while you make the sauce. Skim the fat from the surface of the cooking liquid, then strain it into a saucepan, pressing down on the vegetables in the sieve to extract as much liquid as possible. Put the saucepan over a high heat and boil the liquid until reduced by two-thirds; this will take 8–10 minutes, depending on the size of the pan. Meanwhile, mix together the butter and flour to make a smooth paste.

5] Reduce the heat to low and whisk the paste into the sauce, a little at a time. Simmer the sauce for 2 minutes until slightly thickened. Season with salt and pepper to taste.

6] Remove the pork from the bone in large chunks and serve with the sauce spooned over.

JOHNNIE'S TIP

For crackling, try to keep the fat attached to the skin when removing it. Score the skin with a sharp knife at 3mm/⅛in intervals and put it on a baking sheet. Sprinkle with sea salt and roast for the last hour of the braised pork shoulder's cooking time.

1 tbsp vegetable oil

8 pork cheeks

2 large fennel bulbs, stalks trimmed and
   fronds reserved

1 onion, sliced

1 carrot, sliced

250ml/9fl oz/1 cup red wine

250ml/9fl oz/1 cup vegetable stock

2 thyme sprigs

1 bay leaf

1 star anise

20g/³⁄₄oz unsalted butter, softened

2 tbsp dry white vermouth

1 tsp plain flour

salt and freshly ground black pepper

1 recipe quantity Johnnie's Mashed Potatoes
   (see page 215), to serve

SERVES 4 | PREPARATION TIME 20 minutes | COOKING TIME 2¹⁄₄ hours

PORK CHEEKS WITH CARAMELIZED FENNEL

1] Put the oil in a large cast iron casserole or heavy-based saucepan over a medium heat. Season the pork cheeks. When the oil is shimmering, brown the cheeks for 5 minutes on each side, then transfer to a plate. You may need to cook the cheeks in batches.

2] Put the stalks of each fennel bulb in the pan with the onion and carrot and cook for 5–6 minutes until softened slightly. Pour in the wine and stock and add the thyme, bay leaf and star anise. Nestle the pork cheeks into the vegetables and add a little water, if needed, to cover the cheeks partially. Bring to the boil, then turn the heat down to very low, cover and cook very gently for 1¹⁄₂–2 hours until the cheeks are very tender.

3] Towards the end of the cooking time, cut each fennel bulb into 6 vertically. Melt 15g/¹⁄₂oz of the butter in a large frying pan over a medium heat. When foaming, add the fennel, vermouth and 2 tablespoons water. Bring to the boil, then turn the heat down to low, cover and cook for 8 minutes, turning the fennel halfway. Uncover the pan, turn the heat up to high and cook for a further 2–3 minutes until the liquid has evaporated and the underside of the fennel is slightly caramelized. Flip the fennel over and cook for another 1 minute, then remove from the heat and keep warm.

4] Remove the pork cheeks from the casserole and keep warm. Strain the cooking liquid, then discard the thyme, bay leaf and star anise and reserve the vegetables. Return the liquid to the casserole and boil until it has reduced by about one-third (you need about 250ml/9fl oz/1 cup). Return the reserved vegetables to the sauce to warm through.

5] Mix the remaining butter with the flour to make a smooth paste and whisk it into the sauce, a little at a time. Bring the sauce back to the boil, whisking, then turn the heat down and simmer for 1 minute until thickened. Serve the pork cheeks on top of the caramelized fennel. Spoon the sauce and vegetables over and sprinkle with the reserved fennel fronds. Serve with mashed potatoes.

1½ tsp salt
1½ tsp fennel seeds
2 pork knuckles, each about 1.75kg/3lb 12oz
2 tbsp vegetable oil
2 onions, thinly sliced

250ml/9fl oz/1 cup dry cider
⅛ tsp freshly ground black pepper
1 recipe quantity Johnnie's Mashed Potatoes
   (see page 215) and Wilted Spinach (see page
   218), to serve

SERVES 4–6 | **PREPARATION TIME** 20 minutes | **COOKING TIME** 2½ hours

BRAISED PORK KNUCKLE IN CIDER

Pork knuckle is most often eaten cured as a ham hock, rather than eaten fresh, but this economical cut is perfect for roasting or braising. You will probably need to order it in advance from the butcher, and, if you do, request knuckles from the rear legs as they are meatier than the front legs.

1] Preheat the oven to 170°C/325°F/Gas 3. Grind the salt and fennel seeds together using a mini food processor or pestle and mortar, then mix in plenty of black pepper.

2] Put the pork knuckles on a large chopping board and score the skin at 1cm/½in intervals. Rub the fennel mixture all over the knuckles, making sure plenty gets into the cuts in the skin.

3] Put the oil in a large roasting tin over a high heat. When the oil is shimmering, sear the pork knuckles one at a time until browned all over. Take the tin off the heat, sit the knuckles flesh side-down in the tin and add the onions and cider. Cover the tin with a double layer of foil, sealing it tightly, and cook for 1 hour. Turn the tin around and cook for a further 1 hour until the pork can be pulled away easily from the bones. Remove the tin from the oven and increase the temperature to 220°C/425°F/Gas 7.

4] Transfer the pork knuckles to a baking sheet and return to the oven for 30 minutes to crisp the skin. Meanwhile, bring the juices in the tin to the boil and cook until reduced by half. You may need to add a little water to the tin – there should be around 400ml/ 14fl oz/1¾ cups gravy. Season the gravy with salt and pepper and transfer to a warm gravy boat or jug.

5] Put the pork knuckles on a serving platter and cut the skin and flesh into large chunks. Serve with the gravy, mashed potatoes and wilted spinach.

2 large smoked ham hocks, each about 1kg/
2lb 4oz
750ml/26fl oz/3 cups dry cider
1 onion, halved
1 carrot, scrubbed and halved
1 celery stalk, halved
6 black peppercorns
1 star anise
1 bay leaf
2 thyme sprigs
2 tbsp clear honey

LEEK CHAMP
750g/1lb 10oz floury potatoes, such as Desiree,
peeled and cut into 3cm/1¼in cubes
50g/1¾oz unsalted butter
3 leeks, trimmed and thinly sliced
4 spring onions, thinly sliced
4 tbsp double cream
salt and freshly ground black pepper

SERVES 4 | **PREPARATION TIME** 30 minutes | **COOKING TIME** 3¼ hours

BRAISED HAM HOCK WITH LEEK CHAMP [*pictured overleaf*]

1] Put the ham hocks in a large, heavy-based saucepan. Pour in the cider and top up with enough cold water just to cover the hocks. Add the onion, carrot, celery, peppercorns, star anise, bay leaf and thyme, then bring to the boil over a high heat. Skim away any scum that rises to the surface, then turn the heat down to low, cover and simmer for 2–2½ hours until the meat starts to fall away from the bones.

2] Preheat the oven to 200°C/400°F/Gas 6. Remove the hocks from the saucepan and transfer them to a medium-sized roasting tin. Remove the skin from the hocks and discard. Scoop 200ml/7fl oz/scant 1 cup of the cooking liquid into a jug and whisk in the honey. Pour this over the hocks, then roast for 40 minutes, basting them with the liquid in the tin every 10 minutes.

3] Meanwhile, to make the leek champ, cook the potatoes in a pan of boiling salted water for 15–20 minutes until tender. Drain the potatoes and leave them in a colander for 10 minutes to steam dry. Return the potatoes to the saucepan and mash thoroughly.

4] Melt the butter in a large frying pan over a medium heat. When foaming, add the leeks and cook for 10–15 minutes, stirring occasionally, until very soft. Add the spring onions and cook for 2 more minutes, then stir in the cream and remove from the heat. Put the potatoes over a low heat and stir in the leek mixture a little at a time, then season.

5] Pull the meat away from the ham hocks in large chunks. Serve with the champ.

JOHNNIE'S TIP
Ham hocks can sometimes be very salty and the best way to test this is to fry a small slither of the uncooked ham in a little oil. If it is too salty, then simmer the hocks in a pan of water for 10 minutes. Drain, rinse well, then cook following the recipe above.

1.5kg/3lb 5oz boneless gammon ham, smoked or unsmoked as preferred

1 onion, halved

1 carrot, halved

1 celery stalk

10cm/4in piece fresh ginger, cut into 1cm/½in slices (no need to peel)

6 black peppercorns

2 tbsp Dijon mustard

2 tsp ground ginger

about 15 whole cloves

3 tbsp demerara sugar

1 recipe quantity of Creamy Garlic Potatoes (see page 216)

SERVES 4 (with leftovers) | PREPARATION TIME 20 minutes, plus resting | COOKING TIME 2 hours

HOME-COOKED HAM IN GINGER & MUSTARD GLAZE

The sweet, sticky glaze is perfect for ham, which is wonderful served at a formal dinner, but also makes a great snack. If you like to use a ham on the bone, then reduce the simmering time to 50 minutes per kg/25 minutes per lb. The baking time stays the same.

1] Put the ham in a large, heavy-based saucepan and cover with water. Add the onion, carrot, celery, fresh ginger and peppercorns and bring to the boil over a medium-high heat. Skim away any foamy scum that rises to the surface, then turn the heat down to low, cover and simmer for about 1½ hours. (If your ham is larger in size, then calculate the cooking time as 1 hour per kg/30 minutes per lb.) Make sure that the pan does not boil madly – the bubbles should just gently rise to the surface. Transfer the ham to a large chopping board and let it cool slightly.

2] Preheat the oven to 220°C/425°F/Gas 7. Line a baking sheet with foil. Using a sharp knife, cut the skin away from the ham, leaving a thin layer of fat. Score a diamond pattern in the fat, taking care not to cut into the meat. Mix together the mustard and ground ginger and spread it over the surface of the fat, then stud every other corner of each diamond with a clove. Sprinkle the sugar over the top.

3] Roast the ham for 20 minutes, turning it halfway, until the top is covered in a tangy, sticky glaze. Leave the ham to rest for 30 minutes before slicing and serving with the creamy garlic potatoes. Alternatively, leave to cool and refrigerate before serving.

JOHNNIE'S TIP

Nowadays, most hams have a fairly mild cure so should not be too salty. If you are not sure, however, cut a little piece from the uncooked ham and fry it in a little vegetable oil before tasting. If it is too salty, soak the ham in cold water for 12 hours, changing the water after 6 hours. Drain and rinse, then continue with the recipe above.

ACKNOWLEDGEMENTS

PUBLISHER'S NOTE

The Quick Response (QR) codes included throughout the book will link you to "Show-Me-How" videos, explaining useful techniques to help you with the recipes. The QR codes work best on a smartphone or tablet with a camera resolution over 3MP. If you don't have access to a smartphone or tablet, or have any trouble using the QR codes, all the videos can be found at: www.ibiblios.co.uk/pig

AUTHOR ACKNOWLEDGEMENTS

There are a handful of people I would like to thank in producing this book: Caroline Stearn, without whom this book and its contents would be nothing, Borra Garson (the gatekeeper @ DML), Grace Cheetham, Manisha Patel, Aya Nishimura and the beautiful photography from Yuki Sugiura……Thank you xxx

I'd also like to thank Lord March's Goodwood Home Farm in Chichester, West Sussex, for supplying the most fantastic pork.

PICTURE ACKNOWLEDGEMENTS

Pig illustration: Sailesh Patel
Page 6
Debbie Jones/Imaging Essence
Page 9
[1] Ernie Janes/NHPA
[2] John Eveson/FLPA
[3] Wayne Hutchinson/FLPA
[4] Chico Sanchez/Alamy
[5] Corbis Premium RF/Alamy
[6] INTERFOTO/Alamy
Page 224 (above)
Paul Miguel/FLPA